PENGUIN BOOKS

The Lost Christmas Puppy

Linda Steliou is the winner of Penguin and *Take a Break* magazine's life-story competition. She lives in Surrey with her husband Stephen and several four-legged friends. This is her first book.

The Lost Christmas Puppy

LINDA STELIOU

with PUNTEHA VAN TERHEYDEN

PENGUIN BOOKS

PENGUIN BOOKS

UK | USA | Canada | Ireland | Australia
India | New Zealand | South Africa

Penguin Books is part of the Penguin Random House group of companies
whose addresses can be found at global.penguinrandomhouse.com.

First published 2015

001

Text copyright © Linda Steliou, 2015

The moral right of the author has been asserted

Set in 12.5/14.75 pt Garamond MT Std
Typeset by Jouve (UK), Milton Keynes
Printed in Great Britain by Clays Ltd, St Ives plc

A CIP catalogue record for this book is available from the British Library

ISBN: 978-1-405-91810-7

www.greenpenguin.co.uk

MIX
Paper from
responsible sources
FSC® C018179

Penguin Random House is committed to a
sustainable future for our business, our readers
and our planet. This book is made from Forest
Stewardship Council® certified paper.

For dearest Mamma Rosa

How many years you nagged me to, please, write a book,
Time and again you did so, and gave me a pleading look.
I'd tell you that, while I would truly love to fulfil
    your wish,
To try and write a book would be a different kettle of fish.
Then a competition came about between Penguin Books
    and *Take a Break*,
To write a true-life story, which I entered really for
    your sake.

It was you, for whom I felt sorry when I was not the
    winner,
But, still, you had faith in me, saying my story was
    great for a beginner.
A few months later, I had such a wonderful surprise,
A letter from the Penguin publisher – I could not
    believe my eyes!
Daniel thanked me for my entry, for which he was
    full of praise,
He believed I had potential, and my mind was in a haze.
When we spoke upon the phone, I said, 'I wouldn't
    know where to start.'
Daniel said, 'You have a way with words, Linda, just
    write from your heart.'
You were so thrilled when I told you of his letter and
    his call
That I made up my mind to do my best and give a
    book my all.
After months of typing my story for hours both
    night and day,
The book you longed for is completed. What more
    can I say?
Thank you, Mamma Rosa, from the bottom of my heart,
For encouraging and believing in me, right from the
    very start.
God bless you.

Preface: Welcome to the World

It was 1945 and, while the citizens of London were out in force on the streets, singing, dancing and whooping their celebrations to mark the end of the Second World War, one couple, in particular, had their own special reason to celebrate and cheer.

In a small nursing home, miles away from the bright lights of the city, Bett Peck had given birth to a long-awaited daughter. Now, as Bett gazed down at her beautiful baby, with a head of dark-copper curls, sleeping contentedly in her arms, she knew that the risk she had taken with her own life in bringing this new life into her and her husband Bill's world had been more than worthwhile. In the preceding years, she had suffered the traumatic loss of three babies, two boys and a girl, who had been born perfectly formed but tragically silent.

The doctor had strongly advised Bett to leave her dreams of motherhood behind because of the risk to what they had deemed her 'tired heart'.

But, being the stoic character she was, Bett was determined not to give up on her and Bill's dream. When she conceived again, the doctor said that, to try to avoid yet another sad loss, she needed complete bed rest throughout the pregnancy. In view of the torrent of bombs raining down, with such devastating effect, over London, she was evacuated from her home in Vauxhall to a nursing home in Abingdon, Oxfordshire, which was considered a relatively safe haven.

Now, prizing her gaze away from her baby, her thoughts centred on how relieved and happy Bill would be when he heard the wonderful news of their longed-for baby's safe arrival. 'Please send a telegram to my husband,' she begged the midwife, who, having taken such good care of Bett over so many months and having got to know Bill on his visits, did not need to be asked twice. Smiling, she responded, 'It'll be my pleasure! I shall do it straight away!'

Across the country, Bill unfolded the brown scrap of paper that had just been delivered to his door and, on reading the ten life-changing words printed in block capitals, tears stung his eyes: 'YOUR BABY DAUGHTER HAS ARRIVED STOP MUM AND BABY BOTH WELL'. Bill beamed. He was overcome with pride and happiness as, at long last, he was a father. He literally jumped for joy and, before he knew it, his legs were racing out of the front door as fast as they could carry him. He couldn't get to his beloved wife and daughter soon enough.

While patriotic Bill had wanted to do his bit for his country in its fight for freedom against the enemy, he was grateful that, although many miles away from his pregnant wife, he was a good deal nearer to her than he would have been at the Front. He was employed by a meat wholesale company, called Brown and Knight, and the authorities had refused permission for him to go to war: he was needed to prepare and send food supplies to the troops. He was one of the few fathers-to-be at that time who were able to visit their wives in the nursing home.

As the train to Abingdon chugged along, he closed his eyes and said a silent prayer. He gave thanks to God for fulfilling his dream, with Bett and their baby both safe and well, then that the war was over and his friends had returned home to their loved ones.

On Bill's arrival at the nursing home, he was greeted by the midwife who had taken such good care of Bett during her pregnancy and delivered their precious daughter, then sent the telegram – Bill cherished it for the rest of his life, carefully folded in his wallet, which he kept in the breast pocket of whichever shirt or jacket he was wearing, close to his heart. The only thing closer to his heart, aside from Bett, was his beloved daughter.

The midwife was strolling across the hallway, cradling in her arms three tiny babies, who were sleeping after their feeds. She was taking them to the nursery, to be snuggled up cosily in their respective cots, while their mums had a well-earned rest. With her arms full of such precious cargo, she couldn't risk shaking Bill's hand, for fear of dropping them. But what she could do was smile, and smile she did. 'Congratulations, Mr Peck! Now then, which one of these lovely babes do you think is yours?'

3

Bill quickened his footsteps towards her and, in hushed tones, so he didn't disturb those tiny sleeping beauties, he thanked her wholeheartedly for all her help and kindness. Then he cast his eyes over the babies. They became fixed on one in particular: 'The beautiful one in the middle is mine!'

He was right! He wanted to shout it from the rooftops for all the world to hear but, considerate as ever, he controlled himself. Instead he asked if he could hold his baby girl: he had waited so very long for this precious moment. The midwife nodded and, gently, Bill took hold of his child. He stood stock-still, rooted to the spot for a minute or two, gazing down at his snoozing bundle of joy, then handed her back to the midwife and made his way to Bett's bedside. He kissed her tenderly, careful not to wake her, and settled down in the armchair by her bed. It would be a couple of hours before mother and child were awake, but the time did not drag for Bill. While they slept, Bill lived out his daydream wide awake. Silently, he chatted to his wife and daughter, telling them how happy and proud they had made him, and of all the exciting things that life held in store for them together as a family.

When the two most important people in his life awoke, they stirred at practically the same moment, as if psychic powers were at work. Bett knew that her baby was due for her next feed. As she rubbed the sleep from her eyes, the sight of her handsome husband cradling their baby so lovingly in his arms brought tears of joy to her eyes. The baby gave a little yawn and, as the proud father placed her in her mum's waiting arms, Bett said, 'Let's call her Linda. It's such a pretty name and, even if it's shortened to Lin, it still sounds nice.' Bill nodded, but until his dying day, he always called her 'my lovely Linda'.

Bett often said, 'I hate names that can be messed about with and ridiculed. Children can be so cruel at times, and all too ready to make fun of others.' She found fault with so many names that it's a wonder she liked any name at all. Sometimes, her judgements proved correct, and over the ensuing years, Linda herself was relieved that she never had a problem where her name was concerned.

When the day dawned that Bill and Bett were to take Linda home to Vauxhall, they were looking forward eagerly to showing off their pride and joy to their family and friends, who were all waiting, with bated breath, to welcome the oh-so-special newcomer. Among them were Bett's younger sister, Ann, and her husband, Ted, who were destined to become Linda's godparents. They, also, dreamed of having a child of their own. Little did they know then that while, sadly, their dream would never be fulfilled, Linda would fill that gap in their lives: she would come to mean more to them than just a dear niece – they could not have loved her more if she were their own. As for Linda, well, she loved them just as if they were her mum and dad. How blessed she was to have not one but two sets of loving, caring parents.

The Courtship

Bill Peck and Bett Adams had met for the first time, aged seventeen, at the Flodden Dance Hall in Southwark. Bill, always smartly turned out, his shoes polished so highly that you could see your face in them, was tall, with thick black wavy hair, big brown eyes and a perfect white smile. He was such a handsome young man that, on a number of occasions, people wondered whether he was related to the famous film star Gregory Peck. Bill, while admitting that he was not related to him, was delighted by the compliment.

Bett, too, paid great attention to her appearance, making sure that her accessories always matched what she was wearing. That evening, she wore a dress patterned with delicate blue and yellow flowers. As her light brown hair was naturally straight, she would use rollers and Kirby-grips overnight so that during the day it had waves and kiss curls. She didn't like wearing a lot of make-up and applied only a little face powder and a touch of pink lipstick – never red, which she thought 'common'.

She, too, was likened to a well-known film star, Myrna Loy, and when Bill spotted her across the crowded dance-floor, he did a double-take. For all his good looks and his happy-go-lucky nature, he was relatively shy when it came to approaching the opposite sex. However, as he watched Bett chatting with her friends, and throwing her pretty head backwards in laughter, he knew that, somehow, he had to conquer his nerves and get to know her. As if in a trance, he found himself weaving in and out of the dancing couples, and before he knew it, he was standing right next to the object of his desire.

Bett turned to the handsome stranger standing beside her. Little did Bill realize that, in that instant, she was as mesmerized by him as he was by her. Taking a deep breath, he straightened his shoulders and hoped for the best. He smiled as he held out his hand and said, 'Good evening. May I introduce myself?' Bett felt a blush rising in her cheeks, as she nodded. 'My name is Bill Peck, and I should be honoured if you would grant me the pleasure of the next dance.' Gosh! What a weight that was off his chest!

To his relief, Bett returned his smile and, placing her hand in his, said, 'My name is Bett, and I should be delighted to.'

They joined the other couples on the floor and waltzed to 'I Met Her In Monterey', completely oblivious of anyone else. They spent the rest of the evening together, discussing their likes and dislikes, and getting to know about each other's families – they both came from large ones so that took up a lot of the conversation.

All too soon, it was time for Bett to go home. Bill offered to escort her safely to her front door and, after just a sixpenny bus-ride, they were there. They had enjoyed a wonderful evening in each other's company, so when Bill plucked up the courage to ask Bett out on a date, she accepted without hesitation. For him, that was the icing on the cake.

One date led to another, and another, and their courtship progressed. A year after their first meeting, they became engaged, and three years later, on 4 June 1933, they wed at St George's Church in Borough, London. Bill, such a handsome groom, gazed adoringly at his new wife, who looked every inch the beautiful bride in her long white gown. Her father, also named Bill, was more than happy to give his daughter to Bill in marriage because he knew that she would always be loved and taken care of by the man he looked upon more as a son than a son-in-law. It was a large wedding as they both had so many relatives, and a thoroughly enjoyable time was had by all. Bill's older brother, Harry, summed up the occasion: 'The name Peck stands for this: P for Posterity, E for Energy, C for Courage and K for Kindness.'

The Newly-weds

As Bill and Bett were settling into married life, something happened that would change its pattern for several years to come.

They were only twenty-one and had been married for just three months when Bett's father, at the age of forty-three, found himself having to care for his other five children on his own. Without hesitation, Bett and Bill opened their home and their hearts to them all. As their home comprised just two rooms, it was no mean feat to accommodate eight people but, family being of prime importance to them, they somehow managed to accomplish it.

Eventually, Bill's mother found them a new home, with more rooms, so that they were no longer under each other's feet or treading on one another's toes.

With Bill at the meat firm and Bett working full-time as the manageress of a fur company, Bett's sister Ann, aged fourteen, took on the role of 'little mother' and, in her out-of-school hours, while her friends were meeting up and having fun, she was kept busy doing the housework and cooking, helped by their youngest sister, eleven-year-old Marie. Ann certainly never felt like Cinderella, whether she was sweeping out the ashes when the coal fire had gone out or doing any other household task. As a scholar, she was particularly good at English and history. Later in life, she admitted that she would have loved to become a teacher but she hadn't minded missing the opportunity to study for it because her family meant so much more to her.

Ann's older brothers, Billy, the eldest at twenty-three, and Albie, at eighteen, were the first to go out into the big, wide world. Billy thanked his brother-in-law for all his kindness, help and hospitality, saying, 'They're my brothers and sisters, Bill, but I could never have done all that you've done for them. God bless you, and Bett, too.'

Bill Peck patted him on the back. 'It was our pleasure, Billy, and we'd do it all over again, if need be.' He meant every word.

One day, on his way home from school, nine-year-old Harry, Bett's youngest brother, tripped in the road and was run over by a bus. He was so badly injured that it was thought he might lose his leg, if not his life. He needed so many major operations that he spent eighteen months in hospital. Throughout all of that time, not a day went by when one or other of his family was not at his bedside, praying for his recovery and providing him with all the support he needed to see him through. What a wonderful day it was when Harry was discharged. There was jubilation all around and the family threw a welcome-home party to celebrate his return and the fact that the doctors had saved his leg. He was left with scarring, withering and a limp, but that was a small price to pay after such a terrible injury.

Little 43

When I was nine months old, Mum and Dad had moved from Vauxhall to Raynes Park which, compared to the bustling streets in the heart of London, was quiet and peaceful.

Now I was two years old, waiting patiently beside Mum, clasping her hand, on the kerb outside our home.

'Look right, then left, and right again, Linda,' she said.

We scanned the road for traffic but there was none. It was safe to cross. Mum always kept a hawk-like eye on me, so scared was she that I might run into the path of an oncoming car. It seemed unlikely, given that she'd taught me well how to cross the road safely and we lived in a quiet residential area, without many cars passing through.

Within a few steps, we were over the road and at the front door of Aunty Ann and Uncle Ted's home. They lived opposite us in what they called Little 43. It was one of the happiest homes I knew.

I bounded up to the door and Mum rapped on the knocker.

I heard voices within.

'Darling . . .'

'Yes, darling, I'm going.'

The door swung open and Aunty Ann, my mother's sister, greeted us, arms opened wide. I resisted the urge to jump into them. Mum was already annoyed with me for some reason and I daren't risk winding her up any more.

Mum explained: 'I'm sorry to bother you again, Ann, but ever since she got up this morning, Linda's been tugging at my apron and saying, "I want to go to Ann's house."'

Ann stifled a laugh.

Mum went on, 'Like a long-playing record she was. The only way I could quieten her down was by bringing her over to you.'

I couldn't resist any longer. I let go of Mum's hand, jumped over the door frame and collided with Aunty Ann's legs. Her arms wrapped tightly around me. 'Oh, Bett!' she said to Mum. 'How many times do I have to tell that you never need to apologize for bringing Linda over to Ted and me? She's no bother and we love having her here with us, you know that.'

'Yes, yes,' Mum said, dismissing us with a casual sweep of her perfectly manicured hand.

She went back across the road and I stayed at Aunty Ann's all day, opening cupboard doors or getting under her feet as she cooked and sang in the tiny kitchen she loved. I liked nothing more than when she lifted me up and popped me on to the counter next to her.

My feet swung in the air as I watched her peel, chop and hum her way around the kitchen, but I felt ten feet tall.

Uncle Ted, a gentle man who, like my father, had warm eyes and a big heart, worked at the printer's. He usually left home at eleven a.m. and was back again by five so I saw a lot of him as well as Aunty Ann. Every morning, Uncle Ted would carry the two frail men he referred to affectionately as the Golden Oldies from their bedrooms upstairs to the living room downstairs. One was Old Joe, their landlord, and the other Granddad Adams – Ann and my mother's father.

Old Joe was unsteady on his feet and Granddad Adams, albeit young enough to be Old Joe's son, was weak and had difficulty breathing. It was a sad reminder of the mustard-gas poisoning he had suffered during the First World War. I was too young to understand what had happened but I knew it had been terrible.

Quality Time with Aunty Ann and Uncle Ted

Before Uncle Ted left for work, he would sit me on his lap and tell me a story. He didn't need a book. He was just a wonderful story-teller, changing the tone of his voice and his expressions so that he brought any tale to life in a way that tantalized my vivid imagination.

Although *Cinderella* was my favourite story to read, the one I most enjoyed Uncle Ted telling me was *Little Red Riding Hood*. He spoke softly when he was being Little Red Riding Hood, who hadn't realized that the big bad wolf had eaten her grandmother and was tucked up in her bed, wearing her night-cap: 'Grandmother, what big eyes you have!'

Then Uncle Ted's voice would deepen. 'All the better to see you with!' he'd say, in a chesty growl.

As he uttered these words, he would open his eyes wide, as I gazed up at him, my eyes even wider, in anxious anticipation of what would come next. Just as my heart was about to burst through my ribs, he would grin, squash me to his chest and say, 'Well, my love, did you enjoy that?'

When Uncle Ted went off to work, Aunty Ann took me under her wing. She enjoyed gardening and it was from her that I got my love of all things bright and beautiful. It was a small garden but she planted the borders with all manner of flowers and shrubs, so that, whatever the season, something colourful was in full bloom. I especially loved the lilac in late spring. As its white and lavender clusters came out, the air filled with a sweet fragrance.

In the summer, Aunty Ann and I would sit under the apple tree that grew at the far end of the lawn. She'd bring with her from the kitchen a basket of sandwiches, apples and ginger biscuits. Under the shade of her little tree, we'd have a picnic, just the two of us.

Every now and then, to my delight, she'd produce a letter from her sister-in-law Lil, who was married to Uncle Ted's brother, another Bill. Aunty Ann always saved Lil's letters for us to read together. In them, Lil talked about her daughters, Jenny and Pam. They lived far away and we didn't see them more than once or twice a year so the news from Lil was a welcome treat.

Secretly I had another reason for loving Lil's letters, and Aunty Ann must have known what it was because she often skipped the adult chat at the beginning and read me the bits about Lil's dog. Paddy was a black mongrel with white paws, a playful little chap, who loved having his tummy tickled and going for walkies. Lil had trained Paddy to be her extra ears, as she was hard of hearing: he barked whenever anyone knocked on the door and would find Lil if she was in the garden. There, he would walk around her feet to signal that they had a visitor. I could just imagine the little lad circling Lil and leading her to the door.

How wonderful it would be to have a little dog of my own to circle my feet! Not, perhaps, because I was hard of hearing, but because he loved me so much.

When the time came for Paddy to go to 'God's garden', Bill took Lil to a kennels to choose a new pet. She picked out a coral-coloured Dachshund (a 'sausage dog'). He was with his mum, brothers and sisters and, although he was very small, he managed to waddle over to Lil and lick her hand, whereupon she knew he was the one for her. His pedigree name was Mason Jitterbug so, their surname being Mason, they took this as a sign that he was The One. They named him Pepe and he, like Paddy, was playful: he loved to chase balls and his rubber bone. When the family were in their living room, throwing his bone down the hallway, his little legs used to go nineteen to the dozen as he tried to stop himself sliding on the rug but he always came back for more. When Jenny and Pam were walking home from work, Pepe would be running down the street to welcome them. As he got to within five feet of them, he'd bark, 'Welcome home!' then race back to announce to Lil and Bill that they were on their way.

During the 1960s, there was a huge police presence when the World Cup trophy went missing. The house next to Lil and Bill's was empty but one day they heard a lot of noise coming from over the fence. Pepe could only see the policeman's helmet over the fence and, curious, walked up and down with him. The policeman went to jump over the fence into Lil and Bill's garden, but stopped halfway, one leg in each garden, when he saw Pepe charging up to him. He quickly jumped back into next door's garden and shouted for someone to remove the 'ferocious animal'! When Pam went out into the garden and picked Pepe up, she laughed when she saw a six-foot-tall, burly policeman. To think he was scared of a little sausage dog! Luckily, the policeman saw the funny side and laughed as well. He stayed for a cup of tea, but still kept his distance from Pepe.

I was enjoying listening to all this, when Aunty Ann read a 'newsflash'. There was a fairly high wall between Lil and Bill's garden and that of the house which backed on to theirs. Pepe used to run full pelt up the mound of earth by the wall, which he leaped over to woo Sheba, the Alsatian who lived on the other side. Because Sheba was so large and Pepe was so small, it was felt that nothing could happen between them. Wrong! Lo and behold, Sheba became pregnant by Pepe and, in due course, he became the proud father of Alsatian-Dachshund pups! Oh! Was there a chance that my mum might let me have one, I wondered. She'd always said no before. How could she not be tempted? Again, to my sorrow, she stuck to her guns, and I had to stick to my hope that, one fine day, I would have a puppy of my own. When that day dawned, I would love it and treasure every moment we spent together.

When we weren't in the garden, Aunty Ann and I would have just as much fun indoors. She would clear the kitchen worktop and out would come flour, eggs, butter, dried fruit, nuts, a sieve, the scales, then various pots and pans. By the time she'd pulled out the sugar, I to amuse yourself?' They always gave me their time and, in so doing, made me feel special. More importantly, they did not make me feel I was a nuisance. I was more at home there than I was in my own house.

As the months passed, I noticed something about Granddad Adams. Even with Uncle Ted's help, he was struggling to navigate the stairs and no longer had the strength to come down in the mornings or at any other time. Instead, I went up to his bedside, held his hand and began to chatter about what I'd been doing with Aunty Ann and Uncle Ted. I felt as if I was stepping into Uncle Ted's shoes, telling a story to Granddad. I changed the expressions on my face as I described how we'd baked the cake for Uncle Ted. Granddad looked up at me just as I gazed up at Uncle Ted, eyes full of interest. Then they would close and he'd drift into sleep.

I'd stay for a while, listening to his laboured breathing. I felt sad when I realized that Granddad Adams didn't have long left in this world. My eyes would inevitably stray to the image hanging above his bed. It was a photograph of an angelic-looking choir-boy, holding a lit candle, and, for some reason, it always calmed me. With Granddad's hand firmly in mine, I'd pray silently, *Please, God, don't let Granddad die while I'm sitting with him.*

God answered my prayer.

A week or two later, Mum came into my bedroom one morning, her hair perfectly done, but her eyes red. She perched on my bed and placed her hand on mine. 'Granddad has gone to Heaven,' she said. She patted my hand, stood up and left, gently closing my door behind her.

I got up and dressed, brushed my teeth and combed my hair, all the while tears streaming down my face. Then Mum, Dad and I went across the road and into Aunty Ann's house. Her face showed the sadness we all felt, but somehow her sorrow seemed heavier. Family and friends dropped in and out all day to pay their respects to Granddad, whose body was in an open coffin in the front room; they all offered sympathy and support. He had been such a lovely man and many mourned his passing.

Poor Aunty Ann was devastated at the loss of her beloved father but she was unable to shed a single tear. More significantly, her body reacted in a manner that set the seal on any hope she still had of conceiving a child. Later I would learn that she never had another period. At the age of thirty-four, the shock and grief of Granddad's death sent her into early menopause.

At first, I couldn't pluck up the courage to step forward and look at him. Eventually, though, I inched my way forward towards the coffin. My first reaction was not of fear or horror: I was simply startled not to see Granddad in his pyjamas. Instead, he was smartly dressed in a suit, white shirt and tie. He looked peaceful, just as he had when he'd fallen asleep with his hand in mine. The only difference was that there was no rattling sound coming from his chest. I half expected him to wake up and smile at me. I felt desolate at losing him, but pleased that at long last he was resting comfortably.

In the years that followed, Mum voiced her disapproval of young children attending a funeral, let alone seeing the deceased, so I'm surprised now that she allowed me to see Granddad Adams after he had passed away. But I'm so glad she did.

I said my goodbyes and touched Granddad's face. It was stone cold. I knew then that he wasn't coming back.

Every Sunday that followed, Aunty Ann and I went to Granddad's final resting place in God's garden. Together we placed plants around his grave, said a prayer, and had a little chat to him, telling him what we had been up to. Some might consider it macabre to spend time regularly at a person's graveside, but I found it a comfort. I sensed Aunty Ann did, too, and I was grateful that she took me.

Mum never went. When I asked her why, she said that she couldn't bear to think of her father down there, in the cold dark earth, and would want to dig him up. Although I understood and respected her reasons, I didn't share her view. Instead, every time I tended the flowers and plants at his grave, I thought back to the day I'd said goodbye to him. I pictured Granddad sleeping peacefully and wrapped up warm because I knew in my heart that his soul was in Heaven, where he belonged.

Winter gave way to spring, and the pain of losing Granddad eased. I remembered him fondly. But for

Aunty Ann, the pain continued. The sparkle had left her eyes and, though she welcomed me to her home whenever I appeared at her door, it was as though a light in her had gone out. I struggled to understand the depth of her grief, until I imagined how I would feel were I to lose my own beloved father, how unbearable it would be. I daren't even think about it. Instead, I tried to put the sunshine back into Aunty Ann's life, the way she always put it into mine.

Then one day Dad had an idea. He told Mum over Sunday lunch: 'I think Ann needs a bit of a distraction. What do you think about her working a few hours with me during the week?' He had left the meat business and now had a greengrocer's.

Mum thought it was a great idea and so did Ann.

The very next week, Ann began at Dad's shop. He left home early, at three fifteen a.m., to go to Covent Garden for the freshest fruit and vegetables, and Aunty Ann left for work at six thirty. Whatever the weather, she took two buses, a train and another bus to get there. She swept the floors – especially in winter, when the open front meant extra dirt – cleaned the shelves, boiled the beetroot and topped the Brussels sprouts. She served customers all morning, then headed downstairs to prepare lunch. In the cramped cellar, Aunty Ann would make delicious meals for Dad and his two workers.

Sometimes Dad's friend Alan Fleming would pop in too. It was on one of those occasions, at half-term, that I happened to be in the shop, about to have lunch.

Alan was the local bobby on the beat and always had stories to tell.

That day, he began, 'I was a young copper, struggling to apprehend a drunk outside the shop, when your dad came out and asked, "Are you all right, pal?" Still grappling with the drunk, I shouted, "No," and your dad rushed over to help me restrain him. From that moment on, your dad and I have been best pals.'

Aunty Ann listened with a smile on her face, then served up lunch. She filled our bellies with piping hot stew, and throughout the winter, she produced every belly-warming dish you could hope for on a bitterly cold day.

I was pleased for Aunty Ann. Her smile had returned and her shoulders were no longer hunched with the sadness of losing Granddad. But her new happiness had one other consequence that didn't please me so much. Her working hours meant that when I dashed home from school for lunch she was no longer there. Loneliness seemed to spread through me like poison.

First Visit to Father Christmas

One early morning a few weeks before Christmas in 1947, my mum came into my room and pulled back my covers. 'Come on, Linda, it's time to get up. We have a long day ahead of us. Your dad and I are taking you to see Father Christmas!' I sat bolt upright, already wide awake. Mum was sitting on the side of my bed, smiling. 'I don't suppose I'll need to ask you again to get up!' Of course she didn't! I'd swung my little feet to the floor before she'd finished the sentence! I was so excited that I would happily have scurried off to meet Father Christmas in my pyjamas, dressing-gown and slippers. Nevertheless, Mum got me washed and dressed and insisted that I sat down and ate my breakfast porridge.

As soon as I'd finished Mum helped me into my new outdoor clothes: a beige hat, a beige coat, with a neat little brown collar and six brown buttons, and a pair of shiny brown shoes. Then Dad stepped forward with my brown gloves. Once they were on, the front door was opened and, Mum and Dad each clasping one of my hands, we stepped on to the pathway. Overnight, there had been a flurry of snow, which had settled but would soon melt in the sunlight.

We caught the train from Raynes Park station to Waterloo, then travelled on the Underground to Bond

Street. We stepped out of the station into Oxford Street and huge crowds of people laden with bags, no doubt containing gifts and goodies for their families. There were lots of children about, and I wondered if they were going to see Father Christmas, too. If so, I thought, we'd better hurry: if they were all going to ask him for a real puppy, like I was, I might not get one! Dad picked me up and sat me on his shoulders for the walk to the shop. High above us, strung from lamp-posts, the Christmas lights blazed: Father Christmas, reindeers, sleighs, snowmen, bells and garlands. And that wasn't all – the shop windows were decked out with festive scenes. I saw Father Christmas on his sleigh, pulled along in the snow by his eight reindeer, Cinderella, Little Red Riding Hood, Aladdin and other characters from my favourite stories.

We stopped outside one of the biggest shops and Dad lifted me carefully off his shoulders. 'Well, my lovely Linda,' he said, 'here we are at Selfridges, and this is where you're going to pay your first visit to Father Christmas in his very own grotto! ' He and Mum took my hands and we went inside. As we approached the escalator that would take us up to the grotto, Dad picked me up again, but this time, he held me in his arms.

When we joined the queue of children at the grotto, I hoped the little girls would ask Father Christmas for dollies and tea-sets, and that the boys would want trains and cars. I didn't care what they asked for, so long as it wasn't a puppy because that was all I wanted.

At last, it was my turn. When I went into the grotto, Father Christmas was sitting on a large ornate gold chair, like a throne, on a dais, surrounded by tall, ornate gold pillars, beside the largest Christmas tree I'd ever seen. I remember trying to clamber up on to the dais but it was too high for my little legs so Dad lifted me on to it. Father Christmas was wearing a floor-length red robe and hood, both trimmed in white fur, which complemented his white hair, moustache and long, bushy beard. He lifted me on to his lap, smiled and asked me what my name was. I told him, and then he asked if I'd been a good girl all year. I said I had been a *very* good girl. What would I most like him to bring me for Christmas? As I looked up into his twinkling blue eyes. I told him, 'What I would love more than anything for you to bring me this Christmas, please, is a real puppy of my very own.'

'Ho! Ho! Ho!' Father Christmas chuckled. 'Most little girls and boys ask for several gifts. Is there anything else you would like?'

I replied, 'No, thank you. I have dollies but I can't play with them like I could play with a puppy. If I throw a ball, a dolly can't fetch it back, but a puppy would, and we could be real friends, running around together.'

Father Christmas said, 'As you've been a *very* good girl all year, and you are the only child who has asked me for a real puppy, I'll do my best to make your wish come true.'

Because he was so kind and I was the only child, out

of many, who had asked for a puppy, I was convinced that I would soon have one of my own.

He lifted me down, then held my hand while the shop's photographer took a picture of us together. My first visit to Father Christmas had been captured for ever.

A week or so later when the photograph arrived at our home, Dad showed it to all the family and his friends. One of them, an artist named Wally Bland, said, 'Oh, Bill! What a lovely photo! Please may I borrow it?'

Assuming that Mr Bland wanted to show it to his own family, Dad, beaming with pride, said, 'Of course, just so long as you promise to take good care of it.'

'I will.'

When he returned the photograph, he had kept his promise – *and* had transformed it into a masterpiece! In those days, photographs were mostly in black and white: Mr Bland had painted it to bring it to life. Every year at Christmas, that photograph had pride of place in our home and still does. Later, Dad had the photograph enlarged, copies printed and framed, and told me, 'I've had one done for everyone in the family. They'll all love it and it'll be the best Christmas present they've ever had!'

Cinderella and Prince Charming

I stretched out my legs and sank low into the armchair, then slid off it to the floor.

There, I let out a sigh. With the sizzles and crackles of the log fire beside me and the heat rolling over me, I was in Heaven. It was Christmas Eve and I was looking at the colourful pictures in my favourite book, *Cinderella*. Every so often, I glanced at the fire, the flames flickering and dancing, picturing Cinderella clearing out the ashes once the grate was cold.

Mum was in the kitchen, preparing to serve one of my favourite winter stews. I could smell the vegetables and the pearl barley dumplings wafting through the house. The delicious aroma had been tantalizing me for hours. The minute hand on the clock seemed to be going backwards. Would Dad ever get home so we could eat? Just then, there was a metallic scrape as key entered lock and he came in.

I leaped to my feet and was about to run into the hall to give Dad a kiss, when his voice stopped me in my tracks. He must have thought I was upstairs because he called to Mum, 'Wait until you see what I've got for our lovely Linda. She's going to love it!' Mum's footsteps moved from the kitchen to the hall.

Excited, I wondered if Dad had been bold enough to

buy me my longed-for puppy. I stopped in my tracks, eager to see my present but not wanting to spoil Dad's surprise. With my ear to the living-room door I tried to pick up clues as to what it might be. There was the rustle of paper, like something being unwrapped. Surely a dog wouldn't be wrapped up.

Well, not in paper. Maybe a cosy blanket. I waited for a tell-tale woof-woof. Nothing. I squashed down my niggling disappointment. There was still time.

Mum and Dad stepped closer to the living room and I nipped across the carpet and jumped into the armchair, picked up *Cinderella* and did my best to look engrossed. How awful it would be if they realized I'd been earwigging.

Dad, ever the gentleman, pushed the door open and let Mum in first. As they came into the room, I leaped from the chair to give Dad his usual kiss. His right arm was open wide and I did my best to ignore the little box – my surprise – tucked under his left arm.

His eyes moved to my abandoned book and he beamed. 'Oh, my lovely Linda, how much you love Cinderella! If the story isn't being read to you, you still enjoy looking at all the lovely pictures.'

I nodded happily, my gaze falling on the box. My heart fluttered. Was that the tip of a golden tail I just saw?

'You see,' he said, turning to Mum, 'it's a certainty that Linda's going to love the surprise I've bought for her.'

Mum closed her eyes for a second or two. 'You two are a right pair,' she said.

Dad crouched and placed the box in front of me. The tip of the tail wasn't the furry waggy one I had been hoping for. It was, in fact, the elegant end of a painted blonde bun.

As Dad pulled it out, two eyes, a nose and a mouth appeared. It was a lady in a dreamy blue dress. Cinderella was appearing before my eyes on the arm of her handsome Prince Charming. She was not the puppy I'd been hoping for but she was beautiful. Dad's eyes were shining as he pushed the box out of the way. He produced a tiny bronze key, put it into Cinderella's back and began to wind her up.

Then he set the figurines on the lino that skirted the carpet and, to a tinkling tune, Cinderella and her Prince Charming began their waltz.

I sat on the floor, mesmerized. It was as if they had glided straight from the pages of my book to take their rightful place dancing in the shadows cast by our fading fire.

Dad put more logs on and the flames roared back to life. I wrapped my arms around his neck and said, 'Thank you.' For now, the aching disappointment that I was not holding my own puppy melted away. There was time for Santa to make things right.

That night I tossed and turned, determined to stay awake. I was desperate to see Santa come into my room to deliver my stocking to the end of my bed. Eventually, my eyelids grew heavy and the darkness washed over me. Next time I woke, hours had passed.

Well, they must have because at the end of my bed I

could see a red and green stocking, packed with presents begging to be opened.

I threw back the blankets and sprang out of bed. My feet hit the floor with a thud and, though the chill of the night swirled up my pyjama bottoms, I didn't care. I burst out of my room and into the one across the landing. 'Father Christmas has been! Father Christmas has been!' I jumped on my parents' bed and scurried up to their end. As I wedged myself under the covers, they knew sleep was no longer an option.

Dad planted a kiss on my arm, now close to his face as I tried to get comfy. Then he got out of bed. He fetched my Christmas stocking and a sack, which had been on my bedroom floor, both overflowing with so many gifts that I couldn't have carried either of them. Mum and Dad's double bed was the perfect place to open them. It was cosy, it was spacious. Just right.

Dad rearranged the flannelette sheets, thick woollen blankets and pretty eiderdown around us. Then I began. There were many oohs and aahs as I opened each festively wrapped parcel. I was extremely lucky in that I always received almost everything I had asked for. That year was no exception. Dollies, board games, clockwork toys, Fuzzy-Felt, a yo-yo and a spinning top to name but a few. There were always plenty of annuals and books, including *Noddy*, *Sooty* and *Rupert Bear*. One after another, I unwrapped my goodies. I felt so lucky to be spoiled like that. But it didn't stop the weird aching in my chest. As the bags emptied, my heart twisted. Where was my puppy? Hadn't I been good all year round? Santa was punishing me for some unknown reason. I kissed and hugged my parents, then went back to my own bed.

There, I wiled away the morning buried under a mountain of books. Too young to read them, I lost myself in the pictures, determined to silence the sadness inside me. Once more, the puppy I yearned for had not been delivered. Neither would it be.

In the years that followed, the pattern would remain the same. Except that I could now read all the books. One year, Father Christmas had also brought me a lovely double pram with decorative covers suitable for winter and summer, plus two identical dollies with dark brown wavy hair. As it was winter, they were dressed in thick tights, woollen dresses and knitted cardigans. One was clad in green, the other red. I couldn't wait to show them off. While Mum set to work in the kitchen with our turkey dinner, Dad helped me take my new pram outside and we began a familiar walk.

We soon arrived at the home of Aunty Marie and her husband, Uncle Fred. They cooed over my new 'arrivals' and treated me to chocolate. When I'd shown Aunty Marie my dollies' spotted summer hats, ready for the hot days hopefully to come, we returned home, where Dad roasted chestnuts on the fire until the turkey was ready. Joined by Uncle Ted and Aunty Ann, we tucked into the most delicious of dinners.

Christmas had been very nearly perfect. If only I'd had a wet nose resting on my thigh, hoping and waiting for scraps of turkey. If only.

Christmas with the Pecks

That Christmas was unusual: most years we celebrated Christmas Day and Boxing Day at the home of Uncle Bert and Aunty Lou. They had a lovely large house in the affluent area of Upper Tulse Hill. At the time, they were the only family members able to afford luxuries, but Uncle Bert never forgot his roots. His parents had worked hard to provide the best they could for their ten children and, although there were no expensive gifts, there were always good meals on the table and the house was full of love, warmth and laughter. Uncle Bert carried on those old-fashioned family values with friends and acquaintances. His door was always open and any visitor made to feel completely at home. At Christmas, especially, it was just as well that he and Aunty Lou had such a large house: they invited so many of their family and friends that a smaller one would have been bursting at the seams.

One Christmas in particular stands out in my memory. As ever, upon our arrival, we were greeted with the usual hugs and kisses, but it was Ricky's welcome that I looked forward to most. Ricky was a black poodle that Uncle Bert idolized. He had a son and a daughter but he thought of Ricky as his child, too, and Ricky looked upon his master as his dad. Uncle Bert would be singing and Ricky would tilt his little nose skywards and join in. What a duet! I loved it when Uncle Bert serenaded Ricky, sitting on his lap, with 'Sonny Boy'. Ricky would gaze up at his 'dad' and I felt sure he understood every emotive word.

Watching them enjoy such quality time together made me yearn all the more for a puppy of my own. At one point in the past, Uncle Bert and Aunty Lou had returned home to find their house had been burgled. Uncle Bert's first words were, 'I don't care what they've taken, just so long as they haven't hurt my Ricky!' His first priority had been to find his dog, and how relieved he was to discover him! He was hiding in a corner of the sitting room, behind a large armchair, and although he was shaken by what had happened, he had come to no physical harm. Uncle Bert swept Ricky into his arms and clutched him to his chest, whispering reassuring words of comfort while tears of relief trickled down his cheeks.

Back to Christmas. A friend of Uncle Bert's owned an Alsatian that had recently given birth, and when he offered me one of its beautiful puppies, snow white in colour, I was overcome with joy. At long last I would have my heart's desire. With all the excitement going on around us, everyone greeting one another and looking forward to wining, dining, a good old sing-song and dancing, I was sure that Mum wouldn't say no. Sadly, she did. Suddenly, to me, it felt as though the lights in Uncle Bert and Aunty Lou's crystal chandelier had gone out and that the laughter and the music had died away.

Dad, having witnessed my heartache at being denied that puppy, which I'd wanted to name Snow White, had drawn me to his side and was giving me a comforting hug when, suddenly, Uncle Bert said, 'Bill and Linda, I'd like to introduce you to Nick.' A stranger was standing beside him. Dad shook Nick's hand and wished him 'a very happy Christmas, pal', while I, holding back my tears, managed to take a leaf out of my dad's book and smile. Dad continued, 'So, Nick, how do you know Bert?'

Nick smiled. 'It's probably best that I let Bert explain.' Well, now, my interest was piqued.

Uncle Bert cast a glance at Nick, who gave a nod so slight that, had you blinked, you would have missed it. It was as if he was giving Uncle Bert the go-ahead.

Uncle Bert said, 'I was homeward bound from the office when I spotted this young man busking in the street. It was snowing, bitterly cold, and he was strumming away on his old guitar. I reckoned that the poor soul must be frozen to the marrow, so I made him an offer.'

He offered to accommodate the busker at his and Aunty Lou's home over the Christmas period, during which time he would be able to relax in hot baths, have a nice clean bed to sleep in and consume as much food and drink as he wanted. He would be kitted out in new clothes and given some much-needed money. The only thing Uncle Bert asked of him was that he would entertain everyone by playing his guitar. Although a few relatives could play the piano by ear, and took it in turns to tinkle the ivories each Christmas, this year they, too, would be entertained.

Still sad about the Alsatian puppy, I'd got the story a bit mixed up. 'I liked hearing how kind Uncle Bert was to the busker, but how do you come into it, Nick?' There were titters all round and I realized I'd missed the point. I flushed.

Nick replied, 'I was that busker on the street, strumming my old guitar, and what your uncle did for me was the kindest thing I've ever experienced. My name might be Nicholas, like the saint who comes at Christmas time, but your uncle will always be my very special saint, God bless him.'

Soon, we took our places at the dining-table and Nick sat opposite me. I watched as the feast was laid out before us. We tucked in, and I wondered when Nick had last had a decent meal. He had a huge appetite so I guessed it had not been for a very long while.

When we'd finished, Dad said, 'That meal reminded me of one Christmas I had as a child.'

We all paid attention, knowing Dad was the best storyteller of all. He explained that his mum – we called her Grandma Peck – would have cauldron-sized saucepans filled with her delicious stews simmering on the range, and there was plenty of drink available for those who enjoyed a tipple. They would sing their hearts out to good old London songs, such as 'Maybe It's Because I'm A Londoner', 'Underneath The Arches' and, of course, no Londoner's party would be complete without 'Knees Up Mother Brown', 'The Hokey-Cokey' and 'The Conga'.

Having set the scene, Dad continued, 'The kitchen ceiling used to bow under the weight of everyone dancing in the room above it. It's a wonder it never caved in.' He laughed and we did too.

Then Dad said, 'The Pecks had a chicken they named Old Mary and while Grandma Peck had her for the purpose of laying eggs, we became so fond of Old Mary that we not only looked upon her as a pet but as one of the family, to the extent that she had her own little chair in the kitchen. One Christmas Day, Grandma Peck set to work with her usual gusto. She had promised her children an extra-special Christmas dinner that they would never forget and it was well on its way. She couldn't wait to see their faces.

'While we were all used to the tempting aroma of her delicious meals, such as lamb-in-the-dough, toad-in-the-hole, stuffed hearts, stews and boiled beef with carrots, the smell wafting through the kitchen was new to us.'

Dad related how Grandma had laid the table with plates of vegetables, all spaced around the main dish in the centre. When she called that dinner was ready, Dad and his brothers and sisters rushed in and sat down. 'We were chatting away when we suddenly realized that a certain chair was vacant. We scoured the kitchen for Old Mary, and when our eyes fell on the main dish, the truth dawned on us.'

I gasped. 'Old Mary!'

Perhaps I had expected Dad to shed a tear, but he was laughing. 'Well, we promptly lost our appetites, burst into tears and nobody would take a "peck", so to speak. Of course, Grandma was not best pleased, announcing that, had she known what their reaction would be, she could have spared Old Mary and continued to have her eggs.'

'So what happened next, Dad?' I asked.

'Well,' he said, 'where Old Mary had previously laid her eggs, she herself was laid to rest. We took two logs from the wood-pile and made a cross to mark her resting place. As we stood around it, saying a little prayer, Grandma's annoyance turned to pride.'

'What for?' I probed.

'Pride that her children were so kind-hearted they put their feelings for Old Mary before their own,' he said. 'That Christmas Day may not have been memorable for the reason Grandma had hoped, but she never forgot it. Her children had reminded her by chance that it was the season of goodwill towards all men, even though Old Mary was not only female but also a chicken!'

As we cleared the table, Nick told me what a wonderful family I had and that, no matter how long he lived, he would never forget the kindness and generosity bestowed on him by Uncle Bert, Aunty Lou and their relatives, each of whom had made him feel so welcome.

That made me think. All my life I had been praying and begging for a puppy but here was a man who at Christmas didn't even have a warm home to return to or a decent meal to eat. It pushed things into perspective.

As the partying got under way, Nick picked up his guitar but as he began to play there was a snap, a twang, and all the strings broke! Poor Nick looked mortified. But any worries he might have had that he would be thrown out on his ear were soon banished.

Aunty Ann and Uncle Harry took it in turns at the piano, and our would-be entertainer ended up being entertained!

Not Too Young at All

In latter years, my cousin, Harry, and his wife, Lily, lit up Christmas in more ways than one. But to go back to the beginning . . .

Harry and Lily were each other's first and only love but, because Harry's parents, Charlie and Ginny, felt that they were too young to get married, the teenagers went to court to obtain permission to set the seal on their love. With permission duly granted, Harry and Lily were wed.

In the years that followed, they were blessed with three sons and several grandchildren, and they formed a very close-knit, loving family. The door to Harry and Lily's lovely bungalow was always open wide, not only to their nearest and dearest, but to everyone they knew; all were greeted with welcoming hugs and made to feel right at home.

Their love grew even deeper as the years passed by and, on their extra-special golden and diamond wedding anniversaries, they marked these with two wonderful celebrations, to which they warmly invited their numerous relatives and friends. On both occasions, the same large venue was decorated with banners and balloons, there was plenty of food and drink, and great entertainment was provided by a band.

At their golden anniversary celebrations, rainbow-coloured strobe lights floated across the guests as they danced the night away beneath a gigantic silver glitter ball, which hung from the centre of the high ceiling. At one point the band's singer politely requested that the dancers sit the next dance out, to have the pleasure of watching the hosts take to the floor.

Harry, tall and handsome still, and Lily, with her beauty and figure which women half her age would envy, both looked at least twenty years younger than they were. And, they, equally, possessed youthful characters full of fun, and were a joy to be around. Harry took Lily by the hand and led her on to the centre of the dance floor. The band struck up again and the singer began the perfect song as Harry took Lily into his arms and they started to dance. A hush fell across the room as everyone watched them glide across the floor. They gazed into each other's eyes, just as they had on their wedding day all those years ago. Now, bathed in the gently flickering strobe lights, with the silver glitter ball twinkling like stars above, Harry and Lily looked, for all the world, like the stars of a romantic film. And, as I took in this lovely scene, my mind travelled back to my childhood, and I thought of that special figurine of Cinderella in the arms of her Prince Charming, which my beloved Dad had brought for me, and how they had glided across the floor, too.

It was as if Nat King Cole had written his song with them in mind as they sang along to his words about not being too young to be in love.

As the saying goes, there wasn't a dry eye in the house.

All too soon the evening drew to an end. Harry and

Lily thanked their guests for having joined them on such an auspicious occasion, and for all the lovely cards and gifts which they had received and which they would forever cherish. Likewise, their guests thanked them for such a memorable evening, which was rounded off when Harry, with one arm draped lovingly around Lily's shoulders, gently pulled her close to his side. He expressed how grateful he was to her for all the many happy years which they had enjoyed together, and he wished he could find the words to adequately describe just how large her heart was. The highlight (or, perhaps, I should say, 'high light') of the evening for Lily, I think, must have been when Harry suddenly glanced up at the silver glitter ball, pointed to it and declared, 'You see that great big ball? Well, my Lily's heart is even bigger than that!'

Lily, for once at a loss for words, gazed up at Harry, and her look was testament to the fact that their love had stood the test of time, and that, indeed, they were not too young at all. It really was a memorable occasion for such a memorable couple.

In the weeks leading up to Christmas, Harry and Lily always spent a great deal of time and effort decorating both the inside and outside of their lovely bungalow. As well as the beautiful Christmas tree, which dominated the lounge, there was such a multitude of festive decorations and ornaments that it was just like their very own Santa's grotto. In the front garden, various yuletide figurines were dotted here and there, and the centre of the attraction was a manger, with Joseph and Mary standing beside the crib in which the infant baby Jesus lay. The front of the bungalow was outlined with colourful fairy lights and on the rooftop was an illuminated Father Christmas in a sleigh laden with sacks full of toys, being pulled along by his reindeers, led by Rudolph with his very shiny red nose. The whole scene was a winter wonderland and, when the word spread, people brought their children from far and wide to have the pleasure of seeing it. One of Harry and Lily's neighbours, of whom they were very fond, was a young boy named George, who, sadly, was confined to a wheelchair. Harry and Lily had the bright idea of hosting a special fundraising evening, the donations to be split between George and Asthma Research (Lily herself being an asthma sufferer).

On the appointed evening, Harry dressed as Father Christmas and Lily as Mother Christmas and, helped by their sons and daughters-in-law, they provided plenty of hot Christmas fare, including, of course, traditional mince pies and mulled wine, which they gave out to everyone who turned up. The honour of turning on the lights fell to George, who beamed with delight as he pressed the switch. The waiting crowd cheered as the many illuminations came to life, and carols and Christmas songs rang out. Everyone got into the spirit of things and the night air was filled with happy sounds of merry-making.

I could not help but think, 'If only life could always be like this, with people coming together in harmony.'

The local newspaper took photographs and wrote an article in praise of Harry and Lily's wonderful Christmas spirit.

A Walk on the Wild Side

On one of my dad's rare days off, he took Mum and me in his red car for a day out in the countryside. I was only a few years old, and as full of excitement at seeing hares hopping along under hedgerows and cows grazing in the meadows as adults would be, in years to come, flying thousands of miles to see lions, giraffes, elephants and rhinos living in their natural habitat. Grandma Peck used to say that 'If a herd of cows is lying down, it's a sure sign that it's going to rain. If they're standing up, it'll be sunny.' It was a lovely sunny day, and as my dad drove along the country lanes, chatting and laughing with Mum, I kept my eyes peeled for cows to see if Grandma Peck was correct about their 'weather forecasts'. As we passed field after field full of cows, all standing up, munching grass, I let out a whoop. 'Look! All the cows are standing up and it's sunny, so Grandma Peck is right in what she says! And if they stay standing up, it won't rain!'

Mum had packed a picnic, so, when she and Dad spotted a field full of daisies and buttercups, they thought that would be an ideal spot in which to enjoy it. Mum spread a tartan blanket on the ground for us to sit on – such a pity, I thought, that the pretty little flowers would be flattened. Noticing the look on my face, Mum and Dad cast each other a knowing glance and laughed.

'My lovely Linda', began Dad, 'there's no need to be sad because these flowers are spoiled. After we've had our lunch, your mum has an idea that will put the smile back on your face!' Mum putting a smile on my face? The very thought made me smile. I couldn't get my lunch down fast enough, eager to know what Mum had in store for me.

When we had finished, Dad carried the picnic hamper back to the car and Mum took a little pouch out of her handbag. From it she extracted a tiny pair of scissors, a reel of white cotton and a needle. I didn't have long to wonder what she was going to do with them. She laid them on her lap and began to pick some of the daisies and buttercups that surrounded us. By now Dad was making his way back to us, stooping to pick some of the tiny blooms. He sat down with us. He and Mum indicated that I should hold out my hands, then they placed in them a small pile of daisies and buttercups. Mum said, 'Linda, I want you to watch what I do. If you promise to pay attention and take care with the needle, I shall let you do some, too.' With that, she threaded the needle and slowly pushed it through the daisy stems, one by one, until she had made a necklace. Then it was my turn. I made a bracelet to match the necklace. Then she placed the necklace over my head, while Dad put the bracelet around my wrist. I thought it was the prettiest 'jewellery' I had ever seen, but having Mum and Dad enjoying 'quality time' with me meant more than

A Stitch in Time

We set off again in the car. Suddenly, in the middle of nowhere, we saw a milk depot. Mum asked Dad to stop so that she could buy some milk to take home. Dad said he'd nip into the depot and, of course, I wanted to go with him. We needed to cross the road to reach it and, although the country lanes were quiet with no traffic to speak of, he instinctively took my hand. Mum called, 'Make sure you hold your dad's hand tightly, Linda, and don't run, especially if you want to help him carry the milk, as you no doubt will!' In those days, there were no cartons: the milk came in pint or half-pint glass bottles. Nor were shopping bags provided. Hence, my dad clutched some pint bottles in his arms and, knowing that I loved to help, he gave me a half-pint bottle to hold, and, reiterating my mum's advice to 'be careful', he clutched my other hand in his free one, and we made our way back to the car.

We had just reached the car, when the toe of my shoe caught on the kerb and I was sent sprawling, with the milk bottle. As it smashed, a large jagged piece of glass cut into my right wrist and blood poured out of the wound. Poor Dad let the bottles he was holding slide on to the driver's seat, then swept me up in his arms. Mum practically fell out of the car in her haste to get to me.

Panic set in – we were nowhere near a town where we would find help. My dad removed the glass, and tried to stem the flow of blood with his clean handkerchief, which straight away turned from snow white to bright red. A couple of men, who had been strolling in our direction, ran up to us. They had seen what had happened to me and pointed to a few houses nearby, where they were doing some building work. As if by a miracle, one belonged to a doctor. Because my poor dad was in such a state, one of the men suggested that, rather than waste time giving Dad directions as to which house was the doctor's, he himself would carry me there. Dad placed me in the man's arms and he sped off like lightning, my parents in hot pursuit. Good fortune was on our side, as the doctor was at home. He said I'd been extremely lucky: the glass had only just missed the artery. He cleaned and dressed the wound, advising my parents to take me straight to our own doctor for it to be stitched, thinking that I would be more at ease with him for that procedure. I knew Dr Metcalf well – he had frequently attended my poor granddad and, as was the norm sixty years ago, he was a real family doctor. No matter how busy he was, he always made time for his patients, just as though they were his own family. He was a handsome man, always smartly attired and wearing a bowler hat, and he spoke the Queen's English beautifully.

Needless to say, our trip to the countryside was cut short. When my parents took me into Dr Metcalf's surgery, I remember that, to try to appear brave, I asked him, 'Do you have any children, Dr Metcalf?'

He gave me a beaming smile. 'Yes, I do, Linda. I have six.' To me, an only child, that seemed an enormous number! No doubt my eyes widened in surprise. As he gently inserted the sutures into my injured wrist, he kept my mind occupied by telling me the names of his children and the different things they got up to. My memory of that unfortunate incident is more of people's kindness than the trauma of what might have been, had that piece of glass penetrated my right wrist a fraction deeper.

And, seeing the distress on my mum's face, I was reminded of what Aunty Ann had told me. When I felt unwanted by my mum, Aunty Ann would try to reassure me: 'Your mum does love you, Linda. It's just that she has a funny way of showing it.' Later in my life, I read about a lady who had experienced similar feelings about her mother who, like mine, had suffered a stillbirth. It was suggested to her that her mother seemed detached perhaps because she was frightened of becoming too close to her daughter, for fear of losing her too. That was the most likely, and understandable, explanation.

Our day out in the countryside not only started off happily but ended that way, too.

Mummy's Little Helper

Like most little girls, I wanted to help my mum, but a couple of well-meant attempts went drastically wrong. My 'crimes'? Thinking I was helping, I cut all the red wax off a large chunk of Edam cheese. Mum didn't explain nicely to me that it's best to leave the wax on to keep the cheese fresh. Instead she told me off. With my next plan, I was trying to make up for that mistake: I decided I'd polish the lino that surrounded the carpet in the living room. Mum had already done it, but I thought I'd add my 'personal touch' by redoing it. Taking two clean floor cloths, I knelt on the carpet and began. Having applied a lot of polish with cloth number one, I set about the buffing-up with cloth number two. My little arms were working fast: I wanted to finish the job before Mum, busy in the kitchen, came in and caught me at it, thereby spoiling the surprise. It didn't bother me that my arms were aching because my mind was set on cheering Mum up after I'd spoiled the cheese.

With the lino polished to the hilt, I sat back, chuffed. Mum was bound to be pleased this time, so pleased that she'd forget she was cross about the cheese. Her frown would be replaced with a smile and words of praise.

How wrong could I be? Mum entered the living room just as I was about to get to my feet. 'What are you doing on your knees, Linda? Saying your prayers?' As I stood up, and Mum's eyes fell on the lino, I saw the look on her face. It was not the look I'd been hoping for and expecting. It was the look she'd worn when she'd seen that cheese! What have I done wrong this time? I wondered.

At least Mum had the grace to tell me the lino looked lovely before she said I must never do it again because, having applied so much polish, I had made it dangerously slippery. Most of the floor was covered with carpet and I couldn't imagine anyone slipping on the small amount of lino but, if my luck to date was anything to go by, someone was bound to come a cropper and, worse, it would probably be Mum! From then on, the only time she would find me on my knees was when I was saying my prayers!

Still intent on being Mummy's little helper, I would ask her if I could give her a hand, but she always refused.

'I don't want you to do any dusting, as you might drop something and break it.'

'I don't want you to do any ironing in case you burn the clothes or yourself.'

'I don't want you to put anything away in case you put it in the wrong place and I can't find it.'

She didn't want me in the kitchen with her either: 'It's too small and you'll only be in the way when I'm cooking.' She would add, 'You can do all these things when you're married. You'll have to then', as if she were sparing me household tasks in the meantime. She didn't realize she wasn't doing me any favours. I had to learn the hard way, by trial and error, to do the everyday household tasks that young women whose mothers encouraged them to learn took in their stride.

While Mum always cooked delicious meals, it was thanks to Aunty Ann that I learned to cook. Her kitchen was just as small as Mum's but she liked having me in it with her. I picked up her enthusiasm for cooking and always enjoyed it when I was married and had a kitchen of my own.

Not Guilty!

Considering that Mum felt sure I'd drop something and break it if she let me do any dusting, it's ironic that one day when she was dusting she accidentally knocked an ornament off the mantelpiece. It was a large, beautiful Murano-glass clown riding a bicycle, and it had pride of place among other lovely pieces. As it crashed to the hearth and smashed to smithereens, Mum looked at me blankly and went to fetch a dustpan and brush. She swept up the bits, tipped them into the bin, then hoovered the area thoroughly to pick up any tiny shards she had missed. She never uttered a word. As sad as I was at the clown's downfall, I was mightily relieved that I wasn't guilty of causing it.

On another occasion, when Mum and I had been invited to her sister Marie's home for the day, I was admiring the ornaments displayed on a new fire-surround. There were three shelves on either side and, on each one, there was a pretty figurine or a vase filled with flowers from the garden. On the hearth a shiny black china cat sat, apparently warming itself by the coal-effect electric fire, as a real cat would. I bent forward to take a closer look at it, careful to keep my arms by my sides so I wouldn't knock anything down and break it.

Just then Mum, who had been chatting to Aunty Marie in the kitchen, came into the living room and leaped towards me. She grabbed the cat, as if to safeguard it, and happened to notice that it was cracked. Immediately, she laid the blame at my door! On hearing her raised voice, Aunty Marie hastened into the room to see what the matter was. Mum was urging me to own up to her and apologize for having damaged the cat. I was rooted to the spot. As usual, I was being found fault with, and for something I hadn't done. Tears rolled down my cheeks. Aunty Marie, bless her, set down the tray of tea and biscuits she was holding and took me into her arms to comfort me. 'Bett,' she said, 'Linda didn't break that cat. I did, a few days ago, but as you can only see the crack close up, and I like that ornament, I've kept it. So, please, don't tell Linda off for something she hasn't done!'

As if I wasn't upset enough already, worse was to come. Instead of Mum apologizing to me for the injustice, she said to Aunty Marie, 'Don't make excuses for her, Marie. She has to learn discipline.'

Aunty Marie, having a gentle nature and knowing that Bett was always sure that she herself was in the right, and couldn't be convinced that she was ever wrong, sighed, hugged me closer to her, stroked my hair and quietly reassured me. At least she knew I was 'not guilty'.

Mothers' Day

One year when I was quite a young child and we were out shopping, my eyes fell upon what I thought would be the perfect gift for my mother on Mothers' Day. It was a pretty brooch that depicted the word 'Mother' in violets. I knew Mum loved violets, and that she'd longed for a baby, so I thought she'd be thrilled with this specially chosen gift from her daughter. I was just wondering how to distract her while I spent my pocket money on it when a neighbour appeared in the shop. As the two women became engrossed in conversation, I took the opportunity to make my purchase and pop it into my pocket. At home, as I wrapped it, I envisaged the surprise and delight on my mother's face when she opened it on Mothers' Day.

However, when the day dawned, my mother's smile of anticipation as she carefully unwrapped my gift changed to an expression of such disappointment that I was both upset and mystified. I'd had a vision of her pinning the brooch to her dress, almost as if it were a badge of honour. Instead she rewrapped it and, looking at me as if I'd committed a mortal sin, said, 'Never ever call me "Mother". Just call me "Mum".' She never explained why she'd said that but, as young as I was, I understood from the sad look in her eyes and the equally sad tone in her voice that she had her reasons and, whatever they were, they were so ingrained in her that she hadn't thought how hurt I would be. I never knew what became of that special brooch, but Mum certainly never wore it and I never saw it again. I wasn't angry with her over her outburst, just sorry for the hurt I'd unwittingly caused, especially on that day of all days.

From then on, I was always careful to choose gifts that would make her happy, and cards with loving verses for 'Mum'.

Children Should be Seen
and Not Heard

For reasons I couldn't fully comprehend, my mum would always say she didn't like people popping in and out. We had a lovely little home but she would say, 'Even if we lived in Buckingham Palace, I would still feel the same.' Consequently, I was not the only one who didn't have friends round, she didn't either. In fact, she didn't really have any friends because she didn't go out of her way to make any. She was quite happy when close relatives came to see us, or if they asked us round to their homes. Otherwise she contented herself with an occasional friendly chat with any neighbour she happened to meet when out, or with Alice, who lived in the terraced house adjacent to ours.

She was an elderly lady whom I called Aunty Alice, although she was no relation. Sometimes Aunty Alice would invite me into her house and regale me with stories of the good old days. I loved listening to them and would picture the events in my mind's eye. I especially enjoyed her description of how Raynes Park had been even more countrified before we'd moved there in 1946. From the end of our road onwards, there had stretched miles of open fields and grassland, and the family doctor had made his house calls with a pony and trap. Now there was a bypass, on the other side of which roads, blocks of flats, houses, churches, schools and rows of shops had been built. I couldn't help thinking it was a pity that they'd had to do away with the peace and sense of freedom that comes with the quiet of the countryside.

When Mum and Aunty Alice chatted, they stood on their adjoining front doorsteps, with me between them, not taking in what they were talking about but hoping for a chance to hear more of Aunty Alice's tales of days gone by. After I'd waited quietly and patiently for what seemed an age, I would politely intervene, but the minute I said, 'Excuse me, please,' Mum would give me her admonishing look and say, 'How many times must I tell you, Linda, that children should be seen and not heard?' Nevertheless, I lived in the hope that one day I would be included, just as I always was with Aunty Ann. If I were to have any children when I grew up, I thought, I would never say such a thing to them.

Eventually I would leave them to talk and go up to my bedroom. The only television was in our living room and, there being no computers or video games, which today's youngsters enjoy, I would wile away my time playing board games, such as Snakes and Ladders, or reading. As time went by, I progressed from fairy stories, such as *Cinderella*, *Snow White*, *Little Red Riding Hood* and *Jack and the Beanstalk* to annuals, my favourite of which was *Rupert Bear*, then Enid Blyton's *Secret Seven* series, and books like *Jane Eyre* and *Rebecca*. Door-to-door salesmen were commonplace, in those days, and, when one came round selling encyclopaedias, I was delighted when Mum and Dad bought me the whole set, filled with a multitude of interesting facts and photographs.

When I was on my own, I longed for a puppy's companionship and affection but I could at least lose myself in the wonderful adventures of Lassie, the collie, and Rin Tin Tin, the German shepherd, who starred in my favourite television programmes. As well as being beautiful, they were so clever. I wouldn't have minded if my puppy had neither of those qualities. In refusing my many requests to take me to the place now known as Battersea Dogs and Cats Home, my mum was right when she said, 'I'm not taking you there because, knowing you, you'd want to bring all the dogs home with you. And it wouldn't be just the pretty ones you like the look of but the ugly ones and, especially, the dogs with one eye or only three legs. Your heart would go out to them and you'd want to help them. They're all very well looked after there, Linda, so we'll just leave them be.'

The Icing on the Cake

It was especially sad on my birthday that Mum didn't
like having people round to our house. As at Christmas, I was lucky enough to be given lots of lovely toys,
which I was grateful for and enjoyed, but I missed the
ongoing pleasure of companionship, be it in the shape
of friends or a puppy of my own. Mum always chose
a special 'daughter' card, with loving, heart-warming
words like those I heard from Dad, Aunty Ann and
Uncle Ted, but never from her. She would cook one
of my favourite meals, to be followed by my favourite dessert, blancmange, and there would also be jelly
and ice-cream, tinned fruit, fresh fruit from Dad's
shop, crisps, Twiglets and, in pride of place on the
table, a birthday cake. In fact, there was a real party
spread because Mum was doing her best to give me
a happy birthday. When Dad came home from work,
she would switch off the living-room light and my
cake candles would be lit. They would sing 'Happy
Birthday' to me, then tell me to blow out the candles
and make a wish. No prizes for guessing what I always
wished for!

Unfortunately, in my younger years at least, what I
wished for would never turn out to be the icing on the
cake.

Ramsgate

One of my earliest memories is of an encounter on a beach when I was four years old.

I was perched on a hard seat in our holiday apartment by the window overlooking the sands. My bottom was numb, back aching. I was waiting, watching, and silently begging the storm outside to clear. Finally, a crack appeared in the cloud and the sun shone out.

I turned to Dad. 'Please,' I said, 'can we go to the beach now?'

One corner of his newspaper flapped down and Dad peered out. But he didn't look at me. He stared over my shoulder and through the window. Then it happened. His eyebrow arched up, his brown eyes twinkled and the corners crinkled in the way that told me good news was coming. 'Yes, my lovely Linda,' he said. 'We can go to the beach now.'

Before he'd had time to stand up, my wellies were on and so was my coat. It was inside out and I could only get one arm in, but that was enough to keep it on and it would have to do. There were far more important matters to attend to.

The weather had been terrible and Dad had promised that, as soon as the sun came out, we would go to the beach. I was certain I would burst if he made me stand by the door for another moment. I peered through the screen separating me from the bedroom. A familiar figure with short brown hair was pulling on her boots too. Around her, two extra arms held her in a tight embrace. My father loved my mother dearly. Although I was still so young, I knew I shouldn't be watching them so I averted my eyes and took a deep breath, quelling my longing to scream, 'HURRY UP!'

Finally we stepped outside and the chill of the receding storm burned my face, but I couldn't contain my excitement. We boarded the lift down to the beach, along with twenty or so others. I say 'lift', but it was like nothing I'd seen in the shops at home. Really, it was a work of art. It was topped with a dome and had ornate masonry inside. With a *chug-chug* and a *click-click-click*, it moved slowly down the cliff.

Eventually the doors opened and Mum and Dad stepped out, me in the middle. We walked along the beach. Well, they walked, I ran. I only stopped when my legs were like jelly or when a white shell wedged in the sand caught my eye. I stood with the tips of my wellies in the sea and screamed as the white foam washed over and into them, turning, squealing and running into my father's waiting embrace. He pulled off my wellies and I wandered barefoot.

Hours passed. My parents grew weary and my feet throbbed but I didn't care. Our cheeks were red with the cold but Dad's eyes glowed as he watched me play. I'd waited three days, three whole days – a lifetime – to be on that beach.

Then I came across something that made me stop in my tracks. It had brown fur all over its body, a long, strong face and pointy ears. Brown eyes darted from side to side and, suddenly, the dog pelted towards me, letting out a woofy greeting. I should have been scared, but as he raced up to me, tail wagging, tongue lolling, I let out a hysterical giggle.

The sound must have startled him because he came to a slamming halt, two feet away from me, and tipped his head to one side, as if he was listening for me to do it again. I obliged and he started. He stared at me, tail wagging, head lowered, bum high in the air, apparently about to pounce.

What are you thinking about? I wondered.

A split second later, my new friend was off, barking, racing and rolling around the beach. Next time he returned to me, he had balls of sand hanging from his fur in clumps and as I grabbed for the ones at the side of his face – they were like dangly yellow earrings – a rough hand slipped around mine. 'No, my lovely Linda, don't tug at him,' my father said.

'Why not?' I said, staring at the most beautiful dog I'd ever seen. He was just like Rin Tin Tin, whose adventures I so loved to watch on television.

Dad crouched and pulled me into his arms. 'Linda,' he said, holding his hand out slowly, fingers flopping down, 'this is how you approach a dog.'

Confusion must have been written across my face. But with Dad's slow actions, I saw the dog's attitude change. Cautiously, Dad stretched a hand towards him.

The dog nudged it with his wet nose. He sniffed Dad's hand, once, twice, nostrils flaring, then without warning licked it from wrist to fingertip.

SQUEAL!

Dad looked at me and so did the dog.

'Sorry,' I whispered, clamping my mouth shut.

Just then, a man appeared beside us. 'Tinny, here, boy.'

The dog trotted to his owner and Dad and the man began chatting. I wasn't listening to what they were saying. My eyes were fixed firmly on Tinny as I remarked to his owner, 'He looks just like Rin Tin Tin!'

He gave me a big smile as he replied, 'You clever girl! That's why I named him Tinny.'

What a beautiful boy he was. His brown fur seemed to ripple and shudder as the sun shone on his strong legs and back. I whispered his name and his ears pricked. 'Tinny,' I whispered again. He padded towards me. I held out my hand towards him and waited for him to make a move. He did. As I sank my fingers into his fur, delight raced through me.

It was soft and comforting, just like the teddy bear Mum and Dad tucked under my arm at bedtime when they prepared to read me a story. Except Tinny was warm and smelt like the sea. He butted my hand as if to say, *Don't stop.*

I didn't.

Mum was beside me now and Dad turned to us. He pulled out his camera and bent his knees slightly. Though he was wobbling, he was ready. 'You all look lovely,' he said. 'Now give me a great big smile.' His own smile was hard to resist and Mum and I were soon grinning too.

Click, click, click.

With the moment captured, Dad looked very pleased with himself.

I wrapped my arms around the Alsatian's neck. I was really quite taken with Tinny and it seemed that he was with me, too: he didn't move an inch while I squeezed him.

How wonderful it would be, I thought, to have a dog of my own. One that I loved as much as that nice man loved Tinny. I could run around with him and we could splash in the waves together, or sit in front of the fire and have an afternoon nap.

Tinny had not only made paw prints in the sand that day: he'd made them on my heart.

As Mum lifted me up and away, I brought my lips to her ear. 'Mummy,' I said.

'Mmm?' came the reply.

'Can I have a doggy of my own, please?'

Though she said nothing, I knew the meaning of the sigh that escaped her lips.

The answer was a firm no.

Whether it was the sound of the waves crashing, or my heart breaking, all I knew for certain was that there was a roar in my ears and a flood of tears coming that nothing could stop.

Next day we returned to the beach. By now my tears were long dry and Tinny was long gone. But Mum and

Dad had been coming to Ramsgate in the summer for years before I had arrived and they seemed to know everyone and everything about the place: there was plenty to distract me.

On the beach, I saw a tall dark figure up ahead. Dad greeted him, then introduced me to Johnny. He was a handsome young man, with a kind smile and mischievous eyes.

But I wasn't looking at him. Beside him, an even more handsome figure waited. This one had four legs, a glossy tail and beautiful black hair. He was a magnificent horse. Well, in my four-year-old eyes, anyway. Attached to him was an open-topped red carriage. The sight of it set my heart racing. I pulled Dad excitedly towards it. He lifted me up, over the steps, and I scrambled along the cracked leather seat. Mum and Dad took their places at either side of me.

Johnny flicked the long reins he was holding and, with a jolt, we were off.

I waved to all the people we passed and they smiled back. I felt like a princess and imagined I was Cinderella in her pumpkin carriage, on her way to meet her prince. What a delight.

Unlike yesterday, there were no clouds in the sky, only vast expanses of blue, and hot sunshine to beat down on sunbathers and deck-chair occupants alike.

As our carriage ride drew to an end, I'd already spotted my next adventure. I joined the gaggle of children sitting on the sand and was soon transfixed by the characters in front of me. 'He's behind you!' we shouted, as naughty Punch crept up to Judy. And when the crocodile appeared, ready to gobble them up, we let out bloodcurdling screams, loud enough to make the grown-ups jump. It was a wonderful show but afterwards, boy, did I feel worn out.

Time for lunch.

On the pavement by the beach there were numerous stalls, selling fresh sea-food, such as whelks, cockles and shrimps, then candy floss, toffee apples, lollies and ice-cream. We picked our favourite: the freshest cod with the crispest chips. I enjoyed a side of mushy peas and so did Dad.

When we'd finished, we strolled along the promenade and Dad bumped into an old friend. As my parents and Albert stopped to chat, I dipped in and out of the conversation, eyeing the stalls further down. They were packed with brightly coloured beach balls, buckets and spades to build sandy forts, flags and windmills to decorate them. Well, it was an absolute dream. I didn't think life could possibly get more exciting.

While Dad and Albert continued talking, a man selling balloons happened to come by. Albert stopped him and turned to me with a grin. 'Linda,' he said. 'Choose a balloon. My treat.'

'Ooh, thank you!' I replied, delighted at the prospect.

But there was a problem. I had never before seen such a huge bunch of balloons.

There were animals and hearts and colours galore. I was really spoilt for choice and took for ever to decide.

Suddenly the choice was made – and not by me.

Albert took the whole bunch from the seller, stuffed his hand into his pocket and pulled out a wedge of notes. He gave some to the astonished balloon man and told him we'd have the lot. Then he placed the bundle of strings in my hand and told me, 'Hold them tightly, young Linda, so that none get blown away.'

Dad laughed. 'It's just as well there's not a strong breeze, or my lovely Linda would be soaring skywards with that lot!'

Hours passed and my arms ached. Mum took the balloons from me and Dad scooped me up in his arms. He walked us along the pier, and when the helter-skelter came into view, I knew we would soon be on it. Dad loved the rush of the sea air in his face and the scream of his young daughter as we hurtled down together. My stomach was in knots as Dad carried me up the seemingly endless staircase but he and I both knew that fear would soon be overtaken by excitement.

At the top, he held me tightly and positioned us expertly on a hessian mat.

Though we hadn't yet moved, I was screaming. 'Now, Linda, keep your arms inside mine,' Dad warned. As the mat began to move we let out a whoop. I couldn't tell whose scream was louder, mine or Dad's.

Afterwards we stopped by the funfair stalls and, though I wanted to run from one to the next, with the colour and excitement of it all, I knew better. I stayed close to Mum's side and held on tightly to Dad's hand. I loved spending so much time with my father. He worked such long hours that I didn't always see him before bedtime and never in the morning. He'd be up and away before the sun had risen to his greengrocery. Today he had all the time in the world, and so did I.

When I saw the next stall, I pulled Dad towards it urgently. Behind the owner was a row of shelves and little plastic bags filled with water. They were the best prizes of all.

I looked at him hopefully. He smiled and handed over some cash. The owner bent down and gave me three purple rings.

I aimed. I frowned. Then, with all my might, I threw the first and let out a squeal as it swung around the orange cone and sank to its base. Dad said, 'My lovely Linda, you've only gone and done it the first time round!' With that, the owner reached to the shelf behind him and grabbed a bag. He gave it to Dad, who dropped to one knee in front of me. As he presented me with the bag and kissed my head, I stared at the contents in wonder: a beautiful fantailed goldfish. It swished and jerked in its little home and I couldn't wait to show Mum.

But something stopped me. Surely Mum couldn't stop me taking it home? After all, a goldfish couldn't get under her feet or jump on her lap as she so hated. A goldfish wouldn't need to be taken for a walk either, or provide me with the love and companionship I would get from a dog, but it would be a pet that was all my own.

Mum joined us and eyed my winnings. 'We'll have to get it a nice little tank, Linda.'

I jumped and jiggled so much with excitement that I failed to see the bubbles fizzing all around Mr Sparkle, as I'd decided to name him. Eventually I did, and stopped immediately.

Days later, we were at home again and Mum took me to the local pet shop. Together, we picked out a little plastic aquarium with a miniature coral reef and sunken battleship. I chose green plastic reeds to stick in the pink pebbles on the tank's floor.

I was certain Mr Sparkle would be thrilled with his new home. There were places to hide and things to swim in and out of. What more could a goldfish ask for?

We set it up and I sat for hours watching Mr Sparkle weave this way and that. And when I sprinkled the fish food in, I was delighted to see him rise to the surface to have a bite. Many a night, I watched him until my eyes grew heavy. As my head drooped, a strong pair of arms would scoop me up and carry me towards my room. By the time Dad had taken the first step upwards, I was wide awake but didn't open my eyes. I pretended to be asleep so Dad would take me to my room, slip me gently under my covers and kiss me on the forehead, his cologne wafting over me. In that moment, I was the happiest, safest little girl in the whole world.

Then Dad would creep out and, somewhere on the landing, a chuckle would burst from his lips, hot on the tail of the one that had burst from mine. He had known I was awake, but it was our little joke, and I think he loved tucking me in as much as I loved him doing it.

Teddy

One pleasantly warm day, the sun shining out of a clear blue sky, I wandered into the garden and sat on my red swing. I pushed off and swung back and forth, wondering what my schoolfriends were up to. Were they playing with their brothers and sisters? How I longed to knock on my friend Lesley's door, one road away from mine, and go inside. She was one of six and her house was loud, busy, hectic and perfect. I loved going there. But I was well brought-up, Mum often told me, and it was more than my life was worth to turn up at Lesley's house uninvited. 'Because,' Mum had told me, 'you never know, it might be inconvenient. You *must wait* to be asked.'

So I stayed alone on my swing, gripping the chains and working my legs backwards and forwards, going higher and higher. If I swung hard enough, would I go right over the top of the frame? While I never soared that high, my imagination did, and I used to picture my longed-for puppy on the lawn, his tail swishing from side to side, his eyes following me as I flew higher and higher.

A sudden noise brought me crashing back to reality, and very nearly out of my seat.

I brought myself to a stop, and listened for it again. Agonizing seconds passed. Then I heard it again. *Woof-woof.* I glanced in the direction of those woofs and gasped. A little nose was poking through the missing slats of the dividing fence between our garden and the next-door neighbours', nostrils straining to get a good sniff of what was going on in my garden.

I moved closer and saw that the nose was attached to a little Jack Russell Terrier. He was two shades of chocolate brown with a tuft of white, like a little sock, on his front left paw. He was sitting in the middle of a bed of orange marigolds, next to the fence, peering up at me from curious brown eyes.

As I squatted down and reached out to stroke him, he edged closer to me, and poked his nose through the fence, tail wagging furiously. He licked my outstretched hand and I couldn't contain my delight. I was four years old again, on the beach in Ramsgate. Another squeal escaped me. 'Where have you come from, beautiful boy?' I whispered to him.

Our neighbour, Lilian Groves, came out into her garden. She was smiling and her eyes were as bright as mine must have been. 'This is Teddy, Linda. We've just bought him and, knowing how much you want a dog of your own, we thought you'd be pleased to have him as your new neighbour.'

Pleased? I was thrilled to bits!

I reckon Teddy was just as excited. As Mrs Groves and I chatted, Teddy raced between us, then put his head on his paws and stuck his bottom into the air as if he was about to leap on me. I just knew that he would become my ever so special friend.

I didn't own him but that wouldn't stop me loving

him or him loving me. Love conquers all, as they say. Well, there and then I felt our instant love for one another would conquer the world. When he came to me next, I ruffled his hair and stroked him as he continued jumping and jiggling around me. Then, with a quick word to Teddy that I'd be back, I ran indoors and told Mum about him, a question burning inside me.

She was washing up and stopped when she saw I had something to ask. I let out a breath I hadn't realized I'd been holding and said, 'I wonder if I'd be allowed to take him for a walk?'

Mum's immediate response was, 'If you're asked to, then that's OK with me, but you must go just once around the block, then come straight home.'

If I'd known how to jump up and click my heels, like they did in the movies, I would have done it. Instead I smiled so hard my cheeks ached.

Mum laughed. But she was quick to add, 'Listen to me, Linda. You're not to bother Mr and Mrs Groves about this.' I didn't hear anything she said after that. I'd waited so long for a four-legged companion that I was already out of the door.

In the garden, I found Teddy waiting patiently in his patch of marigolds. It was as if he'd known I'd be back as soon as I could. He let out a woof as I bent down to stroke him.

His new owners, Lilian and Joe Groves, were an elderly couple who had known me since I was a baby.

As Mrs Groves took her washing off the line, Teddy stared at me and I stared at him.

I whispered to him how much we'd enjoy each other's company. 'Maybe I'll be able to take you for a stroll, Teddy.'

He wagged his tail. If I'd had a tail, it would have been swishing in unison.

When she'd finished, Mrs Groves came over to the fence, looked down at my beaming smile and said the immortal words, 'If your mum will let you take Teddy for a walk, Linda, you're more than welcome to do so.'

I could have jumped up and kissed her. 'Oh, thank you so much! I'd love to.' Then I added, 'Mum said I could, providing I didn't bother you.'

She smiled warmly at me. 'It would actually be a great help to us if your mum would let you take Teddy for a daily walk.'

Well, I nearly died of joy.

Mrs Groves spent most of her time caring for her husband, who was quite severely disabled with ankylosing spondylitis: he was unsteady on his legs and had great difficulty in walking. They had helped to fulfil my dream of having a dog to be my best friend so I was only too pleased to help them in return.

Teddy had come into my life just at the right time. With Aunty Ann at work all day, I was often lonely. Now I felt my prayers had been answered.

Mrs Groves shouted instructions over her shoulder as she took her washing indoors.

I didn't need to be told twice. I rushed into the kitchen, told Mum my plan, then raced out of the front door, hopped over the low wall and was waiting for

Mrs Groves when she opened her door. She had already clipped on Teddy's blue tartan lead and gave me the handle.

I thanked her and promised, 'I'll take the very best care of him.'

We set off. It was the first day of the rest of my life.

I made sure Teddy was trotting safely along the pavement in front of the houses, and not on the roadside. God forbid his little legs slip off the kerb and into the path of oncoming traffic. I chatted away to him, just like I would to a friend, and every few yards he would turn his face to look up at me. If he could have spoken, he would have assured me he was still listening, I could tell. We made a great team and it felt like we had been for-ever friends, well, for ever. It was lovely to think we would stay that way.

Before we knew it, we had completed our walkies around the block. As our homes came into view, my steps faltered. I ground to a halt and so did Teddy. He peered up at me, a bemused look on his face. His tail was still wagging but it had dipped and was swishing much slower, revealing sudden anxiety. I bent down and patted his head. 'I know,' I told him. 'I want to go for longer, too. But I can't risk it, Teddy!' It would do me no good to break my promise to Mum: I wouldn't be allowed to take Teddy out again.

I returned him to Mrs Groves. 'Same time tomorrow?' I asked.

She nodded, and my heart soared.

One of Mum's sayings was: 'Don't do as I do, do as I

tell you.' Well, I never saw the fairness in it. Whenever she said it, an image would flash in my mind. One day, when I was grown-up and had children of my own – I often dreamed of two girls with curly brown hair like mine – I would hold them in my arms and shower them with love. I'd tell them about the lessons I'd learned and never utter those words to them. For now, though, I followed Mum's rules. It paid off because I was allowed to take Teddy for his daily walkies.

Every day after school, I rushed home, slung off my schoolbag and ran into the back garden. And every day, without fail, Teddy would be waiting for me in the marigolds. I told him, 'You are a silly sausage, Teddy. Soon those flowers will be gone!' But he did look a picture when he was sitting among them. Not that he knew it. Almost as soon as I'd started speaking to him, he ran off and, judging by the barking and clatter from inside, right through the house. I rushed next door, rang the bell and Mrs Groves appeared. Already Teddy was on his lead, tail going as he waited for me, his walker and best friend. At least, that was what I liked to think.

Over time, Mum let me take Teddy for longer walks and go further afield than just round the block. As the months passed, Teddy and I made our way around the neighbourhood together. I told him everything about my life – school, friends, worries and fears. He was steadfast and loyal in his companionship. Then we started going to Cannon Hill Common, about ten minutes' walk from home.

On our way, we'd get to a main road and my clever

boy would sniff the air and prick his ears. Then he'd sit at my feet and look up at me. He was waiting for my command. Just as Mum had taught me, I told Teddy, 'Look right, look left, then look right again.' I would wrap his lead around my hand twice, losing any slack that would risk Teddy getting overexcited and running into the road, thereby hurting himself or pulling me into the path of a car. When the road was clear of traffic in both directions we'd cross it.

By now, Teddy's trot had become a gallop because he knew we were heading for his favourite playground. The common had lots of open space and soon I'd unclip his lead and let him run free. As we reached the familiar stone balustrades at the start of Cannon Hill Common's lake, Teddy paused for breath. His little pink tongue dangling out of his mouth, he sat for a moment or two and panted. That didn't stop him poking his nose through the balustrade and sniffing the air above the lake. Then he looked up at me and his furry little brows squished together. It was his signal that he wanted to carry on with his walkies.

The two of us paced forward together and the ground beneath my feet and his paws softened. A few yards from the lake, I knelt down, stroked Teddy behind his ears and unclipped his lead. Teddy took off across the common. If he'd had wings, he would have lifted off the ground, the speed he was going. I was thrilled to witness the scene I'd pictured in my mind so many times. At long last, my fantasy was coming to life and unfolding before my eyes.

When people stopped to chat or to pet Teddy, they never asked if he was mine.

They assumed he was, and I was happy to let them think so. Well, it wasn't a lie if I didn't say so, was it? And really it wasn't a lie. It didn't matter that he didn't actually belong to me: his heart and soul were mine just as mine were his.

Time passed, and school became a nuisance to get out of the way. All I wanted was to be with my darling Teddy. Sometimes, when Mum and I returned from shopping, she'd stop and talk to someone on our street. I'd wait patiently while she chatted. Eventually, I'd get fidgety and she would say, 'Stand still, Linda.'

I'd try but eventually I'd be told to go and play in the garden.

Mum didn't have to tell me twice. I'd run up our path, through the front door and out of the back in a flash. Then I'd find the gap in the fence and sit down. Moments later, a wet nose would appear. 'Teddy,' I'd say, 'I couldn't wait to come and see you. How are you?'

He'd woof and wag his tail and all would be right in my world again.

Hours would pass, the sun would set, and I'd be talking to Teddy. Every now and then, I'd say, 'Now, Teddy, are you listening?' He would lift his head off his paws and look at me. *Well, go on then, I'm listening.* Later, my feet tingling from sitting cross-legged for so long, I'd realize Teddy had fallen asleep while I'd rabbited on. It was tempting to lie down and doze by that fence next to my best friend, paw in hand, especially on warm and balmy summer evenings when the sun set late and a warm breeze flowed over us. Instead, I rose to my feet, shook out the pins and needles and said, 'Goodnight, Teddy.'

That was enough to wake him. When he saw me standing up, he knew our time together was over for the day. We'd make our way into our respective homes and get ready for bed. I'd imagine Teddy circling in his and flopping down, resting his little face on his paws. In my bedroom, I wished him goodnight, and good luck, as my father had told me so many times, and wondered if he would dream of me, as I dreamed of him.

In the autumn, the leaves turned yellow, orange and red, then fell to the ground to create an outdoor patchwork carpet for Teddy and me to take our walks on. I reckoned it was his favourite season. He'd shove himself into piles of leaves, pushing through like a miniature bulldozer. What he was looking for, I'd never know! On the common, I'd throw him his favourite yellow tennis ball and he'd run to fetch it. I'd sit on the grass, knowing he'd be side-tracked by something or other before he finally returned to me. When he eventually did, he dropped the ball into my lap, lay down and panted. I'd put my hands behind his ears and give them a good waggle. His eyes would close to tiny slits as his tongue lolled out and his tail swished slowly in the grass. 'That's good, isn't it? Who's a good boy, eh?' Whenever my tone softened, Teddy's eyes would open. *Who are you kidding? Of course I'm a good boy!*

Heads and Tails

Another Christmas party stands out in my memory. That particular year it was held at the home of Dad and Uncle Bert's eldest brother, Charlie, and his wife, Ginny. Everyone was made more than welcome, and a wonderful time was had by all.

Aunt Nell, who was married to Dad's older brother Alf, had taken a turn on the piano, Alf standing by it, while she sang 'Can't Help Lovin' That Man of Mine'. A hush had fallen over the partygoers, as they stopped to capture the romantic interlude, commenting, 'Aah! Isn't love grand?'

With their party-piece over, another figure had come to lean against the piano, and what a figure it was. It belonged to their eldest child, Ellen. She was in her early twenties, tall and slender, with long, dark brown hair that fell in waves past her shoulders. People used to say that she looked like Rita Hayworth, a glamorous film star, and indeed she did.

Ellen was chatting to Aunt Nell, stopping now and then to throw her head back and laugh. As she did so, her hair tumbled and swirled around her shoulders. I was mesmerized. I wished I had long hair like Ellen's. But my wish was to remain just that: a wish. My pleas to Mum to let me grow my hair fell on deaf ears. I thought long hair was pretty but her view couldn't have been more different. She would always say, 'I hate long hair. It always looks a right mess. Ponytails and pigtails are terrible, too – just like rats' tails!'

My bright idea of suggesting to Mum that I should toss a coin – heads, she'd let me have long hair, or tails, I could have a dog – went out of the window. I would have to be patient.

At school I was teased mercilessly because, as far as I was aware, I was the only one taken to the hairdresser's every Friday. I felt embarrassed about that, but Mum would simply say, 'You should be proud that you have lovely thick naturally wavy hair. They're just jealous and not worth worrying about. Ignore them!' That was easier said than done. She added, 'If you have a style that suits you, you should stick to it.' In Mum's eyes, the style that suited me best was called 'the Italian boy', which was short (of course!), with neat flicks of hair framing my face. While I had no say in that matter, a situation arose in which I felt compelled to have my say, no matter what objections Mum raised!

The owner of the hairdressing salon where she took me wanted to put a large photograph of my face in their window, as an advert for their hairstyling techniques. Mum was thrilled to bits. I was mortified. I was already being teased at school – no way did I want to become the object of even more ridicule! The salon was right by the bus-stop several of my classmates used, and I had visions of them seeing my photograph in the window, pointing it out to all and sundry, then taking the mickey out of me. Somehow, I braved Mum's wrath and stuck to my guns. Nothing and no one could persuade me to allow that photograph to be taken, let alone put on display. That said, I would probably have been persuaded if I'd been allowed to have a puppy, but, sadly, that was not an option. In fact, Mum, astonished at what she viewed as my disobedience, wondered if I might make so bold as to turn up one day with a puppy in tow. She said, 'Don't you ever think of bringing a dog home with you, making out that it's followed you, because it'll go straight back where it came from.' The stern look in her eyes matched her tone. That was enough to make me realize she meant every word she had said.

Later, back at home, I couldn't wait to take Teddy straight out for a walk. I told him what had happened and said, 'I'm right, aren't I, Teddy?' He let out a woof, which I took as a sign that he agreed with me. He was my best friend, so he was bound to be on my side.

If only Mum was.

A Very Different Short Cut

Not long afterwards, one of the girls in my class was taunting me about my hair. She launched herself at me and started yanking it. What happened next is so blurred that I can't recall the details, but I walked away from her with chunks of my hair missing. She had tugged it so hard that she'd ripped it clean out.

When I got home for lunch and Mum, as ever, set about brushing my hair before I went back to school for the afternoon, she noticed clumps coming off into the hairbrush.

A look of disgust flashed across her face, then red-hot anger when she realized someone had done it to me on purpose. 'Who did this to your lovely hair?' she demanded.

I was trembling at the knees because I dreaded to think what action she would take if I told her. Without realizing it, the culprit was at war with my mum. Although the girl and I had had our differences, I really didn't want Mum to sort her out. I worried that the girl's mother and then perhaps her father would want to sort *me* out and thus the war would continue.

After much interrogation – I didn't want to be on the receiving end of Mum's wrath – I came clean and told her what had happened. Mum marched me back.

Every step of the way I was hoping and praying that, by some miracle, we wouldn't find the girl, who was blissfully unaware of the telling-off in store for her.

No sooner had we arrived at the main school building, than we saw her heading towards class. I nudged Mum and tilted my head in the girl's direction. In three long strides, Mum was on her. She swung the girl round to face her and admonished her for what she had done to me. She was speaking in hushed tones but I heard her say it was more than that girl's life was worth to come anywhere near me ever again. Then she grabbed the girl's lovely long plaits and pulled them round to the front. With the hair in one hand, Mum reached into her handbag with the other and pulled out a pair of sharp scissors.

The girl's eyes widened and so did mine.

Just above the pretty bows, which were the plaits' finishing touch near the girl's ears, Mum proceeded to cut them off.

By now, the playground had ground to a halt and my face was a shade of darkest beetroot red. Mum held the plaits aloft. 'That will teach you a lesson,' she told the girl, who ran off in floods of tears as I stood rooted to the spot with fear.

I had to prepare to meet my doom, because surely the girl's mother was bound to be as furious as Mum was, perhaps even more so, seeing that her daughter had lost a lot more hair than I had. That night, I couldn't sleep for worrying. Next morning, I confided in Mum.

She said, 'That girl asked for what she got. If she

hadn't pulled your hair out, she would still have her own.'

I went to school, head down, ready to meet my fate. But something strange happened: nothing. To my amazement, the days slipped by without any comeback.

When I told Mum, she smirked. 'I told you so,' she said.

I ended up feeling sorrier for the other girl than I did for myself, wondering if she understood why her mother hadn't leaped to her defence, as mine had to mine. And I had to admit I loved how my lioness mother had protected me, her cub. For once, Mum had been on my side.

Music to My Ears

I was in town with Mum and Dad when I first saw it in the window of a music shop: a beautiful slick radiogram. I already had a small record player, but radiograms were coming into fashion, so-called because they comprised a radio and a gramophone, or record-player.

Sadly, the pet shop where I had looked longingly at the adorable puppies for sale, in the hope that one day Mum would relent and let me have one, had closed down. I had never been allowed to enter the shop to give them a cuddle and had had to be content with peering through the window, my nose pressed to the glass.

Now, as I eyed the radiogram, Dad put his arm around my shoulders. 'My lovely Linda,' he said, 'what are you looking at with such commitment?' I told him and his arms slipped around me. 'Well, in a few weeks, you'll take your eleven-plus exam. If you pass it, I'll buy you the radiogram as a reward.'

I turned to face him, with the biggest grin. 'Really, Dad?' I said.

He nodded.

That afternoon, we returned home early, cutting short our trip around the shops at my request. As soon as we got in, I rushed to my room, pulled out my books and began to revise: maths, English, science, history. All my subjects were now top priority. I had only weeks to go, and if I passed, I'd have not only that beautiful radiogram but enough pocket money saved to buy a Cliff Richard LP. I was in love with him! I practised answering questions, and Dad read what I'd written with me, correcting my grammar and the odd spelling mistake. When he could see I was getting tired, he would put the books down and tell me a story. My favourites were about his own schooldays.

'I remember my teacher was giving a lesson and I found myself on the verge of dozing off. Oh, gosh, I was so bored.'

I giggled.

'So I daydreamed about going outside and playing football. Just as I imagined dribbling the ball towards the goal and scoring a corker, something was said in the classroom to snap me back to reality.'

He was laughing.

'The teacher instructed us all to write an essay on the topic she'd been talking about. The very one I hadn't heard a word of!'

'So what did you do, Dad?'

He laughed until his eyes were wet. 'I didn't have a clue what she'd been talking about so I went home and racked my brains. On Monday I returned to school and handed her the essay. She took one look at it and told me to put my hands out. I knew I was about to get the cane but the look on her face was worth it.'

Dad had written about his grandmother's cat, which had just had kittens.

Finally, the day arrived and I entered the exam hall confidently. Then I turned over the question sheet and let out a defeated sigh. The subject we had to write about was trains.

Trains!

I looked around to see if someone was pulling my leg. But I was met with a hall full of fifty children, heads down, pencils scribbling. I cracked on. I wrote gibberish – I couldn't even remember what I'd put when I handed in my paper.

Three weeks later, I was leaving home for school when the postman arrived. In the pile of letters was the envelope with my results. I pushed it into my bag, only opening it as I entered the school gates. Under my name and student number, there was one little word. FAIL.

That day, I learned everyone in my class, except one girl, Diana, had fluffed the test. It made me feel only a tiny bit better.

At home, Dad suppressed a smile and gave me a reassuring hug. 'Don't worry, sweetheart,' he said. 'You know we love you anyway.'

It wasn't much comfort. After all, love wouldn't bring me my radiogram, would it?

Next day, I came home to find that self-same radiogram in the living room. Dad was home from work early, casually reading his paper in the armchair next to it.

In my haste to get over and have a closer look, I skidded and fell to my knees on the lino. The corner of Dad's paper flapped down.

'Dad?'

He slipped on to the floor in front of me, his back to the radiogram. He smiled at me. Granddad Peck had always said my dad had been born smiling and, looking at him now, I didn't doubt it. Dad tilted his head towards the radiogram. 'It was supposed to be your reward for passing, but you shall have it as your consolation prize instead. I'm sure you did your best.'

Just as I slammed into Dad for a bear hug, Mum appeared in the doorway. She had a tea towel over her shoulder and her hands were covered with white bubbles from the washing-up liquid, but she was wearing a smile to rival Dad's. She watched us for a moment, beaming, then wiped her hands and returned to the kitchen. I felt that she, too, was delighted with the new radiogram. It certainly was an improvement on their old wireless, and its highly polished walnut veneer made it a most attractive piece of furniture.

With Love, Always

It was Saturday morning and I bounded out of bed with the excitement that had been with me since the day Teddy had come to live next door. Every Saturday I would spend two or three hours taking him for walks in the park, swimming in the lake and stopping under the big old oak trees for a rest. That morning, I opened the curtains and my eyes moved to the right as they always did, scanning for Teddy sniffing around the garden next door, when I spotted something strange.

Though Teddy was nowhere in sight, a large hole had appeared at the end of the Groveses' garden.

Then I saw it.

Mr Groves was straining towards the mound of earth with something in his arms.

He couldn't stand up straight so I couldn't see his cargo. But when he reached the hole, he stood sideways on. As the little brown dog with one white sock came into view, I screamed.

My darling Teddy was in Mr Groves's arms. He was floppy and his eyes were closed. I raced downstairs, sobbing, and flew past Mum in the kitchen.

As I burst into the garden and shouted for Mr Groves, I heard a dull thud.

'What's happened?' I called over the fence. 'What's happened to Teddy, Mr Groves?'

There was a shuffling sound and Mr Groves appeared at the gap in our fence. 'I'm sorry, Linda, but we found Teddy this morning. He's dead.'

My mind reeled and my knees wobbled. My hand flew to my throat as I tried in vain to stop another scream escaping. *How had this happened?* Teddy hadn't been ill or weak or showing any signs to alert us that something had been wrong. He'd been as healthy as they come, eating well and going for his long walks with me as usual. How was it that, overnight, something had taken my boy from me?

Mr Groves was trying to comfort me but all I could hear was the roaring of blood in my ears as my heart raced at a manic pace.

I rushed back inside and into Mum's arms. I told her what had happened and she hugged me. Then she let me go and returned to her dishes. I stood for a moment, dumbstruck. She knew how much I loved Teddy. She knew how much attention I'd paid to him and how my affection and care for him had never waned. I'd shown for four years that I would care for a dog properly if only she'd let me have one. Now the closest thing I'd had to a dog of my own was gone and Mum was acting as if I was crying for attention. How could she not tell that my tears were flowing straight from my heart?

I returned to my room and pulled out the beautiful colouring pencils and card I had stashed in a box under my bed – all gifts from Mum. I cut out two rectangles of card, one longer than the other, and fixed them together with string in the shape of a cross. I took my red and pink pens and began to draw.

When it was finished, I went downstairs and waited at the fence till Mr Groves came out again. I showed him the cross and he waved me in. I stood at the mound of soil covering Teddy's body and placed the cross at the foot of the grave. Then I sank to my knees. I promised to remember Teddy for ever and read the words on the cross out loud: *With love always, my best friend*.

Mr Groves and I planted some shrubs around Teddy's grave, which was at the end of the garden near the brick wall separating the Groveses' from the house behind theirs. I reckoned they should have buried Teddy next to the gap in the fence, where he had always waited in the marigolds for me. Whether it was for Teddy's sake or mine that I wished this, I wasn't sure. All I knew was that my Teddy was gone and my heart was broken.

When Dad came home, I rushed into his arms. I sobbed and sobbed and then I cried some more. 'Teddy's gone,' I told him.

He kissed my head, patted my back and soothed me. We stayed like that for a long time, and when finally the sobs had subsided, and I was left sniffling and numb, I pulled away. 'Please, Dad,' I said, '*please* can I have a dog? I don't know what I'll do without Teddy.'

Dad held both my hands in his and squeezed them tightly. 'My lovely Linda. If it was up to me, you'd have a pack of dogs to call your own. But your mum doesn't like animals around her and I can't force this on her.'

His explanation made perfect sense but it didn't help. For a moment I wanted to rant and shout. Mum had had dogs when she was little. She'd grown up with not one but two dogs – a Border Collie called Bruce and a terrier called Buddy. She must have enjoyed having them around – I mean, who wouldn't? – so why was she denying me the chance to enjoy the pet I'd yearned and begged for, and had proved beyond all doubt I would take care of?

'My lovely Linda, maybe when you're older and have your own home, you'll be able to have a puppy of your own.'

I looked up at Dad and nearly laughed. By then, I'd have died from the wait! I was only twelve and a house to call my own was an eternity away. What was I supposed to do until then? Dad wrapped his arms around me. For now, his bear hugs would have to do.

When Monday came, I no longer rushed home from school. Instead, I stretched out the few minutes it usually took. The thought of not finding Teddy, tail wagging and lead waiting for his daily walk, made me want never to get home. But, as always, I did.

That day, I had no tea and went straight to my room. As I so often did, I tried to lose myself in a good book, hoping to drift off to sleep, dream of Teddy and escape the nightmare reality.

The days and weeks without Teddy dragged by. I resisted opening the curtain on the right side of my bedroom window so I wouldn't see the bump in the grass at the back of the Groveses' garden. It signified everything in my life that I dearly loved and wanted so much. Every day I asked Mum for my own dog. She'd give me 'the look', the *don't waste your breath or my time* look. The answer was no and would remain so. If I ever asked her why, she'd say, 'I've told you so many times, Linda, that I don't like animals around me.'

Although we had a black and white cat, Bonnie, I knew what Mum was saying was true. She never allowed Bonnie to sit on her lap or stay in the house for long.

A short while later, I returned home from school one day and found Dad in the living room. He was rarely home so early. He hugged me and took my hand. 'Come with me.' He led me into the garden. When I saw what he was showing me, I let go of his hand and ran over to it. There, gleaming in the sunlight, was a shimmering emerald green bike. It had white handle-bars and a matching seat, with a tartan bag on the back. I mounted it, awestruck that such a beautiful bike was my very own. Dad said, 'Come on, let's take it for a spin.'

I couldn't yet ride a bike without stabilizers so I pushed it out on to the road.

Then, with Dad holding the back of the seat, I climbed on and placed my feet on the pedals. I pressed forward and, with a wobble, I was off. For three solid hours Dad pushed me up and down the road, making sure I didn't topple over. His arms must have ached as much as my legs did. Then he said, 'Right, my lovely Linda. This time I want you to try it on your own.'

I wasn't sure I was ready but Dad insisted.

After a few deep breaths I set off. I swerved left, then right, and resisted the urge to hold my legs out and scream. Behind me, I heard a whoop and a series of shouts as Dad watched me ride my bike alone for the first time. As I got the hang of it and my bike did as I wanted, I felt the breeze ruffle my hair and caress my face. What freedom! Next day, I made for the common on my own, wishing away the tears as I imagined darling Teddy running beside me. It was there that I discovered something while taking a break on the grass: a tiny baby hedgehog. I looked around for its mother or a nest but I could see neither. I waited for a while, debating if I should leave it be. But when it gave a tiny cry and slumped forward, my heart lurched. It had been abandoned and was probably starving and weak.

I gathered up some grass and, using it as padding, scooped the poor mite into my hands, then into the tartan bag on my bike. Surely Mum wouldn't mind my keeping it as a pet. It was so small and needed help. Once my new friend was snug in his bag, I put the lid down and rode home with a smile on my face.

I pulled up outside and called for Mum.

She was out in moments. 'What is it, Linda?' she said, worried. 'Are you all right?'

I told her I had a surprise and motioned for her to come over to the bike, now parked outside the front garden. I asked her to close her eyes. She raised an eyebrow but sighed and did as I asked.

Then I lifted the lid of my bicycle bag. 'You can open your eyes now.'

Well, when she did, they very nearly popped out of her head. She looked at the baby hedgehog and stepped back. 'Get rid of that horrible thing. It's bound to be full of fleas!' With that, Mum rushed back inside the house, no doubt to wash her hands for standing so close to the hedgehog. Hoping that the poor creature hadn't understood what she'd said, I put the lid back down. Keep it as a pet? How wrong I'd been! The least I could do was release it on to familiar territory. I pedalled back to the common.

That summer I turned thirteen and something wonderful happened. For the first time, Mum allowed me to go out, proper out, with my friends.

Teenage Years

A new routine emerged for weekends. On Saturday mornings I met the girls from school on the corner where our roads joined. Then we'd walk to the Saturday-morning cinema performance: they showed fabulous action movies and long-running Western series. Every week, the episode would end on a cliff-hanger, leaving us gripping our seats as the immortal words *to be continued* rolled across the black screen. Then the lights would go up and our chattering begin. Who would survive? Who would escape the baddies? Who would switch sides? It had us speculating all day. My friends and I went on to enjoy films like *The King and I* and *Ben-Hur*. We saw them over and over again, never tiring of the now familiar scenes and lines.

I spent my evenings busy studying in preparation for the summer exams. At the end of the hard slog I'd receive the ultimate reward: after my fourteenth birthday I would be allowed to go to London with my friends. I dreamed of visiting Big Ben, of walking along the Thames in the shadow of Parliament and Tower Bridge. When the time came, my father said, 'Mind how you go, my lovely Linda, and have a good time with your friends.' Dad trusted me: it would never have entered his head that I could do anything wrong.

Mum had a somewhat different approach. Shortly before my first trip into London, she laid down the law. Her ground rules were:

- I must not wear any make-up, other than just a little bit of pink lipstick, definitely not red.
- I must neither smoke nor drink (as if I would!)
- I must not go anywhere of which I knew she disapproved, such as the Astoria Club in Charing Cross Road or the Lyceum Ballroom in the Strand.

'Linda,' she warned me, 'those places are strictly out of bounds.'

I couldn't understand why I had to be the only young adult in London banned from them, but I surmised that Mum didn't want me to grow up too soon.

There were more rules to come.

- I must not talk to strangers and get 'hiked up', as Mum put it, with the wrong sort of person.
- I must stick close to my friends.

Finally, Mum said: 'Linda, you daren't be home one minute later than ten o'clock.'

Really! As if she needed to warn me! I hadn't been a minute late for anything my whole life!

As I pulled on my jacket, Mum issued her parting shot: 'Don't do anything I wouldn't do!'

Well, that didn't leave me with much, did it?

Eight hours later, I got back, having visited Trafalgar Square where all the pigeons were, grabbing lunch at a street market nearby, then catching the Tube and going for a stroll through Hyde Park as the sun set. Now my feet throbbed and my back ached but I'd never been so happy. I put the key into the door, and before I'd got in and taken my shoes off, a figure materialized beside me. I nearly jumped out of my skin. 'I do hope you didn't do anything I wouldn't do.'

'Mum,' I replied, 'of course I didn't.'

'Hmm,' came the reply.

I climbed the stairs and flopped on to my bed. I was exhausted. Hours must have passed when I stirred to the comforting scent of a familiar cologne. 'Ssh,' Dad said, as I called out, half asleep. 'It's only me.' He tucked me under the blankets and planted a kiss on my forehead. He turned off the light. 'You'll have to tell me all about your day tomorrow.'

Next day, I woke to the delicious smell of a roast chicken – and sat bolt upright in bed. It was one o'clock. Lunchtime! I got washed and dressed and made my way downstairs just as Mum was dishing up. As we ate, Mum questioned me about what I'd been up to in London the previous day. It wasn't so much a nice family conversation as an interrogation and it upset me. I'd done nothing to warrant the third degree.

As Mum's uncalled-for questioning continued, I squirmed in my seat and couldn't look her in the eye because I was so angry. Dad's friend had once said that I spoke with my eyes so I tried to keep them off Mum. But when our eyes eventually met, Mum concluded my stare was a sign of guilt and began jumping to conclusions. My emotions bubbled over and so did my tears. I sat silently, having placed my knife and fork back on my plate.

Dad stepped in. 'Leave the girl alone. She's done nothing wrong.'

Now Mum focused on him. She gave him that look, and when that didn't stop his attempts to protect his daughter from the undeserved verbal assault, she went a funny shade of red. 'How do you know what she's done and what she hasn't?'

Dad was silenced.

In the weeks and months that followed, every time I went to London, I pictured Mum's stern stare and Dad's look of love. That was all it took to ensure I behaved myself.

I had no interest in stepping out of line. So we returned week after week to Trafalgar Square. My parents had taken me there as a little girl and the excitement of the pigeons flocking around me, pecking corn – a man sold it there – from my hands, never left me.

My friends and I spent the rest of the day sight-seeing. We stopped outside Buckingham Palace, Number 10 Downing Street and Parliament.

Later, as we walked along the Embankment beside the River Thames, little did I know that soon I would be retracing those steps not as a teenager but as a young woman, strolling hand in hand with a young man at the start of many romantic dates.

Heaven and Hell

In the bustling streets of London, we'd always find a spot to stop for a rest and a coffee, feeling very grown-up and chuffed to bits that we were doing so without parental supervision. It was a wonderful distraction from the loss of my darling Teddy: I still missed him but revelled, as teenagers do, in spending more time with my friends away from home.

Though it was the sixties, with flower power and psychedelic drugs all the rage, we never touched a thing. We were innocent enough to be satisfied with coffee and the wondrous views of London. Independence was the most addictive drug.

At home, Mum warned me to stay away from the 'Teddy boys', as she called them, the teenage boys who frequented the local disco. I wasn't allowed to go there, but sometimes the boys and I crossed paths. I wasn't interested – and daren't be, with Mum the way she was.

It wasn't until a rainy Saturday afternoon in London, two years later when I was very nearly sixteen, that my head was turned. My friend Renee and I had gone to our favourite coffee shop, the ever so swanky 2i's – pronounced 'two eyes' – hoping to catch a glimpse of our favourite pop star, Cliff Richard, who was known to frequent the famous café in Soho's Old Compton Street from time to time. When we arrived, to our dismay, the place was packed. Many of the singing and guitar-playing stars of the fifties and sixties had gone there as unknowns to be discovered by the talent spotters it attracted, which was why it was so popular with us normal folk. But with bodies cramming the place, Renee and I decided to go into the coffee bar next door. It was called Heaven and Hell.

Being good girls, we reckoned Heaven was the place for us. The walls were angelic white and it was brightly lit. The only trouble was that Heaven was already full. I didn't fancy traipsing back out into the bitterly cold wintry weather to find somewhere less crowded so I took Renee's arm. 'To Hell with it!' I declared, descending the stairs with a hysterical giggle.

In Hell, the walls were a dark, rich red and the subdued lighting was in the form of red-eyed devil masks along the walls. But almost immediately everything disappeared from view: all I could see was the devilishly handsome young man sitting opposite the door. He had slick black hair, flawless tanned skin and dark brown eyes I wanted to melt into. He was sitting with a friend, who, by all accounts, wasn't much of a looker.

I turned to Renee and nodded in the direction of the two young men. 'I don't think much of yours,' I said.

We both laughed and ever so casually wove our way across the room. When a chair became vacant next to the handsome stranger, I took it, Renee settling beside me.

For me, this was a bold move indeed. I hadn't a clue as to what to say or do next. Luckily, his back was towards me so I leaned over to Renee and said, 'Now what?'

She shrugged her shoulders and raised her eyebrows. She had no idea either.

How on earth was I going to get to know this gorgeous man next to me?

Just then, the men's conversation paused and my young man turned towards me. He smiled and I flushed. If Dad's friend was right, and I did indeed talk with my eyes, surely he wouldn't need telling of the romantic notions that were circling in my mind about him.

If he noticed, he didn't let on.

Courteously, he held out his hand to shake mine and introduced himself as Stephen.

Renee leaned forward and whispered in my ear, 'Well, you already like the look of him and his name's Stephen – your favourite boy's name. I guess it's settled then!'

Stephen introduced Renee to Tony. He had an accent I couldn't place, and my eyes were drawn to his smile and perfect teeth. Gosh, he really was handsome. As he talked, I was reminded of the film *South Pacific*, which Dad had taken me to see when I was ten.

Stephen had eyelashes so long you could have swept the floor with them and he reminded me of the famous actor Rossano Brazzi, who had played the lead role in the film.

When the usual pleasantries had been exchanged, such as where we lived, what our interests were, I felt more at ease. Soon Stephen and I were chatting the grey afternoon away. I learned he was originally from Cyprus and had come to London four months earlier.

He was studying English so that he could sit in London the electronic-engineering exams that he'd already passed in his hometown. I wanted our friendly chat to go on and on, and was dreading the moment when Stephen would say goodbye.

However, to my surprise and delight, he said, 'Would you like to go with me for a walk by the river?'

Despite my fear of water and inability to swim, I would happily have dived into the Thames with him. I thanked him for his invitation and said, 'Yes, please, I'd like that.' Luckily, Stephen's friend asked Renee if she would like to come with him. If she said no, I'd have had to as well: I couldn't have left my friend alone. With Mum's rule that we must stick together ringing in my ears, I begged Renee with my eyes to do as I wanted.

By now, the evening was drawing in. On leaving the warmth of Hell, the cold night air made us shiver. Unlike a few hours earlier, though, when Renee and I hadn't relished the prospect of wandering around outside, I was viewing a walk by the river in an entirely different light. Especially when Stephen said, 'Can I put my arm around you to keep you warm?'

I smiled and nodded. As his arm went around my shoulders and he pulled me closer towards him, the glow I felt inside more than warmed the cockles of my heart. If only the fires of passion were enough to keep us warm. It was very cold. We made for a sheltered bench, sat down and huddled together. Even though our two friends were beside us, I felt as if Stephen and I were the only two people there. As we watched the river flowing, the lights along the Embankment casting their reflections on the water, we might have been the only two people in the entire world.

Stephen and I chatted away about our childhood and upbringing, what we were doing with our lives now, and what we hoped to do in the future. He had been born in Yialousa, Cyprus, had five younger brothers and a large white dog called Jack. As he talked about playing with his brothers and Jack, I hung on his every word. How lovely it would have been if Teddy and I had had Stephen, his brothers and Jack to play with.

Suddenly Big Ben struck the hour. The chimes told me it was eight o'clock, and jolted me back to reality. I stared at the enormous clock face and wished I could turn back time, if only for a few hours. I couldn't bear the thought of having to say goodnight to the man of my dreams. However, I dared not risk Mum's wrath by arriving home a minute after ten so I forced myself to say goodbye. 'Thank you for a lovely evening,' I began, 'but I'm afraid I have to head for home now.'

Renee jumped to her feet and I turned once more to Stephen. 'I'm late. My parents will be calling out the army to search for me.'

'I'm sorry you have to go,' he said, 'but you're lucky

in having parents who love you enough to care about your being home safe and sound on time.'

It was a kind thing to say.

Stephen and his friend walked with Renee and me to Waterloo station. Every step of the way my heart was beating in a funny way. The way it would beat, I imagined, when you had to say goodbye for ever to someone you loved deeply. At the station the boys waited with us on the platform until the train pulled in.

Picturing myself as the plain fifteen-year-old I was, I didn't think for a moment that Stephen could possibly want to see me again, let alone with romance in mind, so I steeled myself for the goodbye. But something unexpected happened. Stephen reached for my hand and clasped it in both of his. With his eyes fixed on mine, he said, 'Please may I see you again, Linda?'

I was so surprised that I hesitated for a second, wondering if I'd heard right.

'I'd like that very much,' I spluttered eventually.

The train was just about to depart so my friend and I leaped aboard. I pulled down the window as Stephen called, 'Will one o'clock next Saturday here, underneath the station clock, be convenient?'

Convenient? He was truly my very own movie heartthrob!

'That'll be lovely,' I shouted back.

We waved to one another until the train had chugged out of the station.

With a sigh I sank on to the seat, thinking of the final

scene in *Summer Madness* when Katharine Hepburn was on a train, leaving behind the love of her life, played by Rossano Brazzi. That was where any similarity to Stephen's and my situation concluded: it had been the end of their movie romance, but I knew in my heart that this was only the start of ours.

The following weekend could not come fast enough. Any thoughts of studying were out of the window as I counted down the days till I saw Stephen again. I did wonder if he might change his mind and leave me waiting under that clock, like a fool, but I needn't have worried. On Saturday at one o'clock he was there as promised. This time, we didn't hesitate to walk hand in hand as we headed outside into the crisp winter sunshine and towards the river.

The day whizzed by, and this time when we said our goodbyes, Stephen took my telephone number and promised me he'd ring me soon. And he did. We arranged that he would come and pick me up for our next date, and when he did, Dad gave me a wink and went to answer the door. As I checked my hair and powdered my nose one last time, I heard Dad say, 'Hello, my son, how are you?'

Stephen chuckled. 'Very well, thank you, sir, and yourself?'

My heart soared.

At the time, the newspapers were in a frenzy about Cypriot men, saying horrible things about them. But I didn't care where Stephen was from, and I knew that the minute Dad clapped eyes on him, he wouldn't either. I didn't have so much confidence in Mum. Beforehand, I'd told her Stephen was Swiss.

After she'd met him, she laughed. 'If Stephen's Swiss, then I'm Chinese.' She said no more because Stephen was a wonderful, honourable man, and anyone who met him knew it instantly. He and I quickly became inseparable.

One Sunday afternoon, I went across the road to Aunty Ann's for our weekly chat.

'Something wonderful's happened,' I told her.

'Oh?' she said, arching an eyebrow.

'I've fallen in love.'

She took my hand in hers. 'I know,' she said. 'I can tell!'

Stephen and I courted for months but the trek from London every week was a long one and bit into our time together. No sooner had I arrived and we'd had something to eat than it was time for Stephen to escort me to Waterloo and my train home.

One Sunday over lunch, Aunty Ann turned to Stephen. With a twinkle in her eye and a hand covertly squeezing my knee, she said, 'Darling Stephen, we have two spare rooms here now that Granddad and Uncle Joe are no longer with us. Why don't you come and live with us?'

Stephen and I beamed at her.

'That would be great, Aunty Ann, thank you,' he said.

The following week, Stephen moved from north London and settled into Aunty Ann and Uncle Ted's home. I was so happy I thought I'd lose my mind. Now Stephen was across the road, we'd go for walks on the common and trips to the cinema. Like most youngsters in love, we'd sit in the back row, share some popcorn and pay more attention to each other's lips than the screen.

Every time I saw Stephen I returned home zinging with love. How I longed for us to get married.

The Engagement

By now, I was eighteen and we'd been courting for what felt like an eternity.

But we were both starting to get on our feet, me with a job as a shorthand typist, Stephen as an electrical engineer, having gained all of his qualifications in the UK, as his goal had been when we'd first met.

One night, he came to my home to collect me for a dinner date. He was fifteen minutes early and I wasn't quite ready. 'I need to speak to your dad for a moment,' he said. 'Could you wait in the other room, please?'

I made my best nonplussed face and left the living room, with my compact in my hand. Instead of finishing getting ready, I pressed my ear to the door and listened, like the eavesdropping schoolgirl my mother would have despised. Stephen spoke quietly for what seemed the longest time. Then, there was silence, followed by Dad's booming voice: 'Welcome to the family, my son!'

Family? Could this mean . . . ?

Now I heard a hand patting a back, then a rustling that told me the two men in my life were embracing. I could have burst with happiness. This was it! We were getting married!

The next day, Stephen and I chose a beautiful diamond cluster ring for me and, with my parents' blessing, officially became engaged. We were both working full time in good jobs, had the support of our families, and began laying the foundations of our life together. However, I found my job, with the London and Scandinavian Metallurgical Company in nearby Wimbledon, painfully dull. I had reached a point at which I honestly felt that if had to type 'alloys' or 'manufacture' one more time I would scream. When I confided in Stephen, he said, 'So why are you still working there? Let's find you something else.' Together, we scoured the local press and a London paper we picked up one Saturday in town. There I found my salvation: an experienced shorthand typist was needed urgently on Fleet Street.

Fleet Street: the epicentre of British news!

Well, I just had to apply.

Panic Stations

To our delight, I was offered the job on the spot after a fifteen-minute interview. I began the very next day. It meant better pay and a daily jaunt to town, which, to my nineteen-year-old mind, was the perfect setting for the daily grind. I loved going there every day, after the confines of my sheltered life in Raynes Park. In London, the women wore tailored skirt suits, lashings of bright red lipstick, and their shiny hair was swept into gorgeous up-dos. In contrast, I still had my Italian-boy haircut and wore just a little pink lipstick.

The men smoked, swore and rushed about without the gentlemanly chivalry I was accustomed to. I kept my head down and worked hard, determined to succeed. The bustling news room at Reuters, a giant of journalism, was thrilling and daunting in equal measure. The copy that came in was as exciting to hear as it was to type up and pass on and I revelled in feeling truly grown-up at last. I was a working woman with my own money and a handsome fiancé I adored. With Stephen, Aunty Ann, Uncle Ted and all my school-friends within minutes of my home, my life felt very nearly complete.

Soon I became so efficient in my work that I was entered by my line manager into a secretary-of-the-year competition, run by *Woman's Own* magazine. It involved a series of observed tasks and I had been faring well until one of the judges, Marjorie Proops, a well-known columnist and agony aunt, came to stand right behind me, peering over my shoulder.

Though I knew she was entitled to see how I was getting on, I hated being watched at work: it was an annoying hang-up from my days as a young child, unable seemingly to do anything right in Mum's eyes. Lo and behold, Marjorie Proops's scrutiny, and my worry of setting a foot wrong put me off the task in hand. Still, I came second in the competition, a close runner-up. I was chuffed to say the least, and Dad was particularly proud of me.

I'd never been happier until later that year, something happened, which left me crippled with anxiety and limited my life in a way I could never have imagined. It began midweek on an early train to Waterloo. I had a horrible sensation in my stomach and was counting down the minutes till we pulled into the station so that I could dash to the loo. I was certain I had a stomach bug. But, midway between stations, the train ground to a halt in a darkened tunnel. As whispers and questions spread around the carriage, the driver came on the tannoy. We'd broken down.

I had stomach cramps and broke out in a sweat. My heart raced as I imagined everything that could go wrong with the bug raging through my body and the mortification that would ensue if I was unable to control it. Twenty minutes passed before the engine whirred to life. Somehow, I'd clung on to my breakfast and my dignity. Finally we pulled into the station and I rushed to the loo. Thank Heaven I hadn't disgraced myself on the train – or platform! I rang Dad and he came to fetch me. I was ill for the next twenty-four hours.

Although the bug seemed to have left my system, the physical symptoms didn't go away. Every time I got on a train, my stomach lurched and I felt terribly ill. When I saw the doctor, he ordered tests. Thankfully, all the results came back negative. I was immensely relieved and decided to celebrate by treating myself to some new clothes. When I boarded the train at Raynes Park I was full of the joys of spring and looking forward to my shopping expedition. Unfortunately, that joy did not last long. Kingston was only a few stops away, but when the train came to a halt just outside New Malden, I suddenly experienced those same dreadful feelings I had suffered on the journey to Waterloo.

A sensation of impending doom spread up my chest and I began to panic. I stood by the doors and as soon as the train pulled into the next station, even though it wasn't mine, I jumped off. By now, my heart was racing as though it would burst out of my chest. The normal sounds of the world became a continuous ringing in my ears, and my vision blurred as I began to cry.

I flew into the Ladies on the platform, so thankful I'd made it in time. However, to my amazement, the pain didn't come. Nonetheless, I abandoned my trip to the shops. On a prayer that my tummy would behave itself, I caught a train home, thankfully without incident.

The mystifying sensations did not abate. I would be overcome whenever I was on public transport, or even in a car. I couldn't face the anxiety that getting on a train would bring and, reluctantly, I quit my job in Fleet Street just a few months after taking it. I accepted a post as a shorthand typist in Nelson Hospital instead, within walking distance of home. The bus stop was at the end of our road and the hospital only two stops away, but I had become too wary to contemplate that journey.

I was delighted to find my work in the X-ray department extremely interesting. I loved hearing about the different medical conditions. The medical world was fascinating and I knew I'd found my working home there. A few months later, when an opportunity came up to become the maternity and gynaecology secretary, I didn't hesitate to take it. I was doing what I loved, surrounded by little babies and glowing expectant mums. What a bonus!

I found myself thinking more and more about the day Stephen and I would have our own family. His mum begged me to give her a granddaughter. I laughed and said, 'I'll do my best.'

One Sunday lunch at Aunty Ann's, we were all tucking into roast chicken when Stephen took my hand and cleared his throat. A quiet and relatively shy man, his call for attention surprised everyone – myself included. 'Mum, Dad, Aunty Ann and Uncle Ted,' he said, 'you'll be happy to hear we've finally set a date for our wedding.'

Chairs were instantly pushed out and everyone got to their feet, pulling Stephen and me up too. A Spaghetti Junction of arms wrapped around us, and every squeeze told us how happy they were for us. When we'd untangled ourselves, Mum rushed over the road and came back five minutes later with a crisp new notepad. She began to make a list of all the things we had to get done. We laughed at her flurry of excitement. She didn't understand why we were so calm. 'There's so much to do!' she said. 'Two years is not that long, you know!'

My New Friend, Win

Desperate to overcome my fear of travelling, I forced myself to attempt the short bus ride between home and work. As I waited anxiously, alone at the stop at the top of my road, a lady approached and smiled at me. She had a lovely face and twinkling blue eyes. She was around the age of my mum and seemed familiar.

We struck up a conversation and I was soon confiding in her that this was to be my first journey in ages, and the reason why. I never usually spoke about my problem, for fear of being ridiculed, but something about her made me feel comfortable talking about it. She patted my arm and said, 'Don't worry, my dear. Sit next to me on the bus and we'll continue our chat. Before you know it, you'll be at work.' As if on cue, the bus arrived. We boarded and sat next to each other. She told me that her name was Win and that she lived at the top of the block of flats opposite our bus stop.

From then on, Win and I regularly met at the bus stop and soon forged a friendship, neither of us yet realizing how special it would become.

One morning, as we waited together, Win invited me to her flat. The very next day, I took a seat in her neat little lounge, and after a few minutes she joined me, bringing with her a silver tray on which stood pretty bone-china cups and saucers, matching plates and a mouth-watering array of fancy cakes and biscuits.

'Oh, Win! 'I said. 'This is really lovely, but you shouldn't have worried. After all, I'm not the Queen of England!'

She laughed. 'Well, you're special to me, so I wanted to make it special for you.'

Bless her.

Win was old enough to be my mother, and in fact had a son, Tony, who was three years younger than me. She and her husband, Jim, would have liked more children, she explained, especially a little sister for Tony, but it hadn't happened.

When we had finished our coffee, Win asked me to follow her into the kitchen, where she pointed to the window by the sink, then the ground below. 'You see that grassy area which separates this block of flats from the next?'

I nodded.

'Well, years ago, I would stand doing the washing-up and I used to love looking out of the window and watch the children playing on the grass. Often, there would be a few little boys and just one little girl, playing marbles or football together. She had dark brown wavy hair and was always dressed in pretty floral dresses with a matching bow in her hair. She was such an adorable little thing.' Win smiled. 'That little girl was always laughing. I'd look at her and think, If only I had a little girl like that. But as I didn't, I would have to be content with picturing her as mine.'

Win reminded me of Aunty Ann, who had so desperately wanted a child of her own.

On leaving Win's flat, I thanked her for such a lovely afternoon, and invited her to my home a few days later. I already had an idea of how we would occupy our time. When she arrived, I said, 'I don't know how you feel about looking through someone else's photo album, but I wondered if you'd like to glance through mine while I make our coffee?'

'Oh! I'd love to!'

I handed her the photo album and popped into the kitchen, all the while keeping my ears pricked for Win's voice. If she shouted, my theory would be proved correct.

It wasn't long before I heard her call, 'Linda! Please come here straight away!'

When I walked into our living room, Win was beaming from ear to ear, her lovely deep brown eyes alight with surprise, as she pointed to a school photo of me. In the picture I was about six, wearing a pretty floral dress, with a matching bow in my hair. She didn't know it, but Mum had been so organized that even my underpants had matched my dress.

Win pulled the album right up to her nose to study the picture even more closely. 'It was you, Linda! You were the little girl I told you about, the one I imagined was mine all those years ago!'

I squeezed her hand.

I told Win that when I was in her flat and she was telling me about that little girl, I'd guessed it might have been me, because the only children who lived near me were boys and I sometimes went to play with them near the big flats where Win lived. More significantly, as Mum had my clothes made by Aunty Ann's neighbour, whom I knew as Aunty Pidge, the details Win had recalled resonated with me.

The more photographs we looked at of my childhood, the more Win and I happily reminisced, and neither of us could get over the fact that Fate had brought us together in that way. 'Better late than never, eh, Linda?' From that moment, our bond of friendship became closer, as Win looked upon me as her daughter by proxy and I came to see her as another mother figure.

The Wedding Plans Continue

Mum invited two hundred guests and had been flapping for months, trying to get everything perfect for my special day. Every weekend, she'd painstakingly gone into London to bring back swatches of fabric so I could choose the material for my wedding gown and the bridesmaids' dresses at home. My panic attacks on trains had not abated and I couldn't face the Tube at all so Mum, bless her, had done all the leg work for me. She hadn't said a single negative word about it, or grumbled at having to make so many trips on my behalf.

If I ever told her I felt guilty about the situation, she gave me that look and arched an eyebrow. 'Linda,' she admonished, 'you are my daughter and you're getting married! It's my pleasure and my duty. Now stop whining.'

That was the end of that.

Dozens of swatches of white satin and lace later, the chosen rolls were delivered to my neighbour's home to be transformed. I had asked Aunty Pidge to fashion a long-sleeved, full-length white wedding dress, self-patterned with tiny rosebuds. The five bridesmaids' dresses were made from the same material, but in turquoise, and the little page-boy had a white dress shirt and turquoise trousers.

Everything was coming together.

Six months before the wedding, I got home from work to find Mum and Stephen in the living room, poring over sheets of paper. She turned to me. 'Linda, I've heard something wonderful.'

Stephen's eyes were glowing so I knew it was going to be good. 'Well?' I said, unable to take the suspense. 'What is it?'

Mum and Stephen stood up. 'It's easier if we show you,' he said.

With that, he led me out into the street. He turned left and we walked to the very end of our road where we crossed over and Stephen pulled me to a stop on the pavement.

I looked at him blankly. He smiled and Mum squeaked, 'Tell her!' I could see she was milliseconds away from stamping her foot.

Stephen turned me away from the road to face one of the neat terraced houses.

'It's going to be ours,' he said.

'Pardon?' I said.

'The house,' Mum said. 'It's for sale and Stephen's put in an offer!'

Well, I could have cried – and indeed I did when I learned that Mum had overheard a neighbour talking about it going on the market. She'd swooped straight in, got Stephen on board, and together they'd sought out the owners. He had made his offer, bypassing the estate agent and clinching the deal.

I threw my arms around Stephen and, with my chin

on his shoulder, stared at the neat little house that would soon be our first home. It was just up the road from Mum, Dad, Aunty Ann and Uncle Ted. 'It's perfect,' I said.

A week later, we had the keys. If I could have, I would have kept them in my hand all the time, such was the joy of knowing our marital home was awaiting our arrival as husband and wife.

Husband and wife!

Though we wouldn't move in till our wedding night, it didn't stop us working on the property beforehand. When I say *we*, I mean Stephen. He knocked down the wall separating the lounge from the dining room to make one long room. He then demolished the outside lean-to, which would have fallen over if you'd pushed it, and made a doorway at the end of our new open-plan room, which opened into the little hall. From there, one door to the right led out into our back garden, and another into a lovely modern bathroom, which my clever husband built all by himself and fitted out with a turquoise suite. When he had finished applying the turquoise-and-white-veined ceramic tiles, I set out the matching bathroom accessories. How happy we were making the house into our own lovely home.

The previous occupants had boarded up the space under the stairs in the hallway and we decided to open it up again, thereby making the kitchen bigger. I stood by as Stephen ripped the last of the plasterboard off, and then I gasped. Behind that thin wall there was a mountain of junk. From old newspapers to tins of peas, it was packed with rubbish. Why, we wondered, had they not put it in the dustbin? We rolled up our sleeves simultaneously and laughed as we clocked our mirrored action.

We spent hours cleaning it and eventually it was ready for new floorboards. 'We'll have the cleanest under-floorboards in the town,' I told Stephen.

He then repainted and wallpapered every room of our three-bedroom terrace house.

By the time our wedding day arrived, the house was finished. On the eve of the wedding, I left the hospital with a nurse from the ward and waited for the bus. As it arrived, the rain started again for the fifth time that week. 'Look at this terrible weather!' I said to her. 'I'm getting married tomorrow!'

'Tomorrow I'm going on holiday. We've gone away on the same day every year for ten years and, I promise you, the weather's always perfect. It'll be a lovely day tomorrow, just you wait and see.'

I hoped she was right.

Two stops later, I got off the bus, and as it pulled away, I spotted Stephen across the street, waiting for me as he sometimes did when he was home early from work. We strolled to the common hand in hand and breathed in the crisp evening air as the skies began to clear. The grass smelt wet and the scent of soil hung in the air. We didn't say much to each other: the anticipation of our big day tomorrow was almost too much to bear. For a fleeting moment, I thought of Teddy and how much he had loved this gorgeous space.

If he'd still been around, he could have been our ring-bearer . . . Oh, what an image.

Stephen's hand on mine brought me back to reality. He handed me a small black velvet box. 'Tomorrow, when you wake up, open this.'

'Whatever you say, my dearest,' I replied, slipping it into my bag.

We began to walk home, talking through our plan for tomorrow.

Though Stephen's English was by now perfect, I said, 'Tomorrow, when the vicar asks us to take our vows, I'll squeeze your hand when you should say, "I will."'

He nodded.

On my doorstep, I bade my fiancé goodbye, and for the last time, we headed home separately.

That night, I tossed and turned until I couldn't take the nervous excitement any longer. After six years, Stephen and I were finally getting married. At three o'clock, in the wee small hours of the morning, I slipped out of bed and ran myself a bath. It was time to get ready for my wedding. My wedding!

Afterwards, I took the black box Stephen had given me out of my handbag and sat on the edge of my bed. I teased it open and gasped. Inside, I found a dainty gold chain with a pendant. As I lifted it out, my throat tightened. The pendant was in the shape of a bow with two little bells.

Wedding bells! Wedding bells on our wedding day!

By the time the rest of the household stirred and my

bridesmaids joined us, I was half ready. My hair and make-up were done and I was waiting for the pale pink polish on my fingers and toes to dry. The girls helped me into my dress, then left to go to St Saviour's Church with Mum.

Alone, I studied my reflection in the mirror. A wave of disbelief rolled over me. I really was getting married. There was a soft knock at the door and Dad appeared. He looked dapper in his suit and, as always, he was smiling. Today, though, his eyes glistened with tears. 'My lovely Linda,' he said, 'you look so beautiful. You're the best-looking bride in the world.' He handed me a black velvet box. I opened it to find a pair of gold earrings in the shape of tiny bells – to match the necklace Stephen had given me. I choked back tears as I put them on.

We went downstairs, and as we stepped out of the door, there was a tug on my veil. Dad jumped back, staring at his feet as if they'd betrayed him in the most terrible way. 'I'm so sorry, Linda!' he said. I could only laugh as he fixed my veil back in place.

Outside, our neighbours had gathered to catch a glimpse of me and took pictures of us on the garden path. We posed for them, father and daughter arm in arm, smiling proudly.

We took the waiting limousine to the church, and in the porch, I felt jittery. I slipped my arm into Dad's, and as the organist played the oh-so-familiar tune, we paced together down the aisle. *Da-da-da-daaaa* . . . I was shaking so much that, as I stood at the altar, the train of my dress vibrated on the aisle. But when I looked into my Stephen's eyes a calm settled over me.

After Dad had placed my hand in Stephen's and kissed my cheek, he took his place beside Mum in the front row and they both looked fit to burst with pride. We took our vows in front of the packed congregation. As the vicar said, 'Do you, Stephen . . .' my love for Stephen bundled up in my chest, raced down my arms and filled my fingertips. I gave Stephen's hand a squeeze.

'*I will!*' Stephen shouted. Well, there were titters all round as the vicar finished his sentence and Stephen repeated, 'I will.'

With a bemused smile on his face, our best man, dear Uncle Ted, handed my wedding ring to my bride-groom, who then placed it on my finger as the vicar said the immortal words, 'I now pronounce you man and wife.'

Afterwards, we went to the Woodstock Hotel nearby and enjoyed a wonderful evening of food, wine and dancing. As the nurse had predicted, the weather had been perfect all day. Now as the summer heat cooled and the stars began to twinkle in the sky, the party spilled over into the hotel's gardens. As Bud Flanagan sang 'Strollin', our guests joined us in strolling around the garden, each twirling a pretty parasol above their head.

We couldn't have wished for a more wonderful wedding day and would always be grateful to my parents for having given us an occasion we would always look back on with such happiness.

When the last of our guests had left, Stephen and I went to our very first home together. He opened the front door and then, as was the custom, lifted me into his arms and carried me across the threshold.

We kissed and hugged each other in our bedroom, the lights still off. After six long years, he was my husband and I was his wife. We didn't need to say a word, just stayed locked in each other's embrace.

After a while, Stephen gently stepped backwards, taking me with him. As he reached to turn on the light, his other arm still wrapped around me, there was a click. The switch had moved but the light hadn't come on. He opened the curtains and moonlight flooded in. It was then that we both saw it. The light-bulbs in the bedroom and the hallway were gone, and our bed was piled high with towels. We burst out laughing. The pranksters in the family had sneaked in to wreak havoc on our home before the wedding, a tradition in those days.

It's fair to say that neither the towels nor the light-bulbs bothered us that night. When we finally got under the covers and discovered Stephen's work tools neatly laid out on the mattress, well, that did slow us down. Only for a moment, mind . . .

The day after our wedding, the paint still smelt new. For years afterwards, whenever I smelt fresh paint, it reminded me of the morning after the wedding and waking up in that house, our home.

Stephen knew we wouldn't be having a honeymoon because of my travel anxiety but we took a week off work anyway and, the work on the house complete, we tackled the garden. The fine, sunny weather stayed on our side and we enjoyed the hours we spent together, Stephen mowing the lawn, then helping me dig out the weeds and put in a variety of colourful plants and shrubs. For the first time ever, I felt relaxed and really happy. If we'd lived there sooner, maybe I wouldn't have had panic attacks, I thought. Was it because, in my early years, Mum had put me down so much?

I didn't know. All I knew was that my new life as a married woman had begun and I was relishing every moment.

A Surprise for Aunty Ann

Soon after we married, I popped in to see Aunty Ann. She answered the door, not with her usual smile but with a frown and red eyes. I stepped towards her and put my arms round her. 'What's happened?'

As she explained, my heart sank. Aunty Ann and Uncle Ted, unable to have children, had invested their hearts in their cats. First they'd had a black and white called Bruno, who'd lived for fifteen years. Then came Maxie, who was black and as lithe as a panther but sat up and begged like a dog. That always amused Aunty Ann and she adored Maxie, who would take up her favourite spot on the garden wall to await Uncle Ted's return at five o'clock every day. Now Aunty Ann had tears in her eyes as she said, 'Maxie's gone.' She didn't need to say any more. Suddenly I was twelve again, standing in my bedroom, looking out of the window into my neighbour's garden and seeing poor Teddy being buried.

The pain I'd felt that Saturday morning came rushing back. I sat with Aunty Ann as she sobbed for her beloved Maxie.

When she finally calmed down, I left with a heavy heart, wishing I could soothe her pain. I took the longer walk home, which meant I had to pass the shops. It was there that something stopped me in my tracks. I peered at the advert in the window. If there had been a light-bulb above my head, it would have pinged on. It read: *Tabby kitten seeking loving home ASAP.* I didn't have any paper on me so I scribbled the telephone number in biro on my hand and rushed home. I made the call and, later, arrived at the neat terraced house a half-mile away from Stephen's and mine.

The lady showed me into the lounge and there, on a huge, worn green armchair, was a tiny, mewing tabby kitten. I wanted to rush over and pick her up but I resisted. I didn't want to alarm the poor thing. Instead, I took a seat opposite and spoke to the lady, whose cat had given birth to a litter. The tabby was the last one.

The woman said, 'You seem nice but – please forgive me for asking – will the kitten be going to a good home?'

I smiled. 'It'll be loved as much as any child is loved by their parents.'

Whether I was speaking with my eyes, as I'd been told many times, or whether the words I'd said had done the trick, I wasn't sure, but the lady picked up the kitten and placed her in my arms. The little animal started crying but I held her to me until she quietened, then left the house, bound for Aunty Ann's.

When she opened the door, I said, 'Surprise!' I handed over the tiny kitten to a rather shell-shocked Aunty Ann.

For a minute she was silent, open-mouthed. Then she smiled and brought the kitten to her face. As proud as a new mum, she beamed at me, delighted. Then she took us both inside. 'Thank you so much,' she said.

Sasha the tabby kitten was very well looked after. Aunty Ann cooked her meals and was so gentle and loving with her. Nevertheless, Sasha remained one of the most nervous cats I'd ever met. She never wanted to be picked up or cuddled, but that didn't matter to Aunty Ann and Uncle Ted. They looked after her for fifteen years like devoted parents, oblivious to the behaviour of their beloved child.

In the meantime, my good deed hadn't gone unnoticed by someone who loved *me*.

A Little Surprise

One day when I returned home from work, Stephen appeared in the kitchen with a grin on his lips and his eyes twinkling mischievously. I put down my cup of tea. 'I have a little surprise for you,' he said, 'but it's upstairs.'

As he led me to our bedroom, I blushed, imagining what my new husband had in mind! Then he pointed to our bed. 'It's under there.'

I burst out laughing. 'It better not be a gazunder, Stephen,' I said, remembering my grandparents' chamber pots beneath their bed. As I bent to look under ours, I collided with a pink nose and tickly whiskers. It was the pretty face of another tabby kitten. I knew that to scream with delight would scare the poor mite half to death, so with every ounce of my strength, I resisted the urge and slowly reached under the bed. I pulled the kitten out and held him in my arms. 'Oh, Stephen,' I whispered, 'he's beautiful!'

He beamed. 'I knew you'd love him.'

I already had a name for our new addition: LEO – Love Each Other. Stephen knew how much I'd always wanted a dog but the kitten was a better option for the time being. Our house, though lovely, was too small for a dog and, really, with us both working full time, it wasn't fair to take in a puppy. He or she would be alone for hours each day.

There was another consideration. Stephen and I longed to start a family. Now that we were married, it wouldn't be long, I hoped, till we had children. Having talked it over, we had agreed it would be better to have our children before the dog arrived. That way, the puppy would come into our home knowing and accepting that the children already existed and would come first. We both worried that, no matter how well trained and well behaved a dog was, there was an element of risk in introducing a noisy, helpless baby to a territory the dog had already claimed. For now, we were content to have Leo.

I was twenty-three when I realized to my delight – and Stephen's – that I was expecting. We busied ourselves getting ready for the new arrival.

I carried on working at the hospital, determined not to let my anxiety of public transport and, increasingly, being away from our home render me so agoraphobic that I would become housebound as our baby's arrival drew closer. Stephen changed his shifts at work so that he could walk me home from the hospital – we didn't have a car. He didn't want me to slip on ice or snow with our precious cargo on board.

One night, with my due date only a week away, I had a bath and climbed into bed, exhausted. Stephen and a friend were laying our new carpet, patterned with tiny autumn leaves. I had picked it because it reminded me of Teddy diving into the autumn leaves and bringing me little 'treats', like twigs. There was banging from downstairs as the two men fitted the final segment.

At ten thirty Stephen came to bed. I put down my book on natural childbirth and headed to the bathroom. Suddenly I had to grip the doorframe with one hand. Then there was a sudden rush of water between my legs. Quick as a flash, Stephen jumped out of bed, ran downstairs and rushed out of the front door. If I hadn't known he was going to fetch my parents, who luckily had a car, I would have panicked.

Minutes later, there was a screech outside and Dad ran in. He was still in his pyjamas and his hair was sticking up in all directions. If you looked closely enough, there were creases across his face – he'd been asleep until Stephen had roused him.

Dad and Stephen took my arms and guided me down the stairs to where Mum was waiting in the car. Dad drove us to St Teresa's Hospital nearby, a private place run by nuns. I'd saved my maternity allowance to pay the fee to give birth there. Though I worked at nearby Nelson Hospital, I'd decided early in my pregnancy that I wouldn't give birth in those familiar surroundings, in case I were to have a difficult labour and screamed the place down. With hindsight it was a foolish notion as the midwives who I worked alongside would have taken very good care of my baby and me, I'm sure.

Now, as I was shown to a room, my contractions coming thick and fast, I was certain I'd made the right choice. The midwife examined me and told my parents, who were waiting outside the room with Stephen, to go home: it would be some hours yet before their first grandchild made an appearance.

Mum and Dad did as she advised, but she returned to me with a reassuring look on her face. 'Your husband would like to stay with you during the birth.'

I was amazed and so very happy. It wasn't normal practice in the late sixties for husbands to stay with their wives during childbirth but I was relieved that Stephen would be with me during the tough hours ahead. We were led to a room with a deep bath filled with warm water and a built-in seat. 'If you would please take a bath now, Linda,' the midwife said, 'we'll get started.'

'But I've just got out of the bath!' I exclaimed.

She assured me it would help speed labour so I did as she asked, and then I was taken to a bed. As the pain increased, Stephen stood by my side with the gas and air in hand. He mopped my brow with a sponge he produced from his pocket. 'It's a real one from the sea. Someone told me it's the best thing to mop the brow of a woman in labour.'

The midwife and I told Stephen to sit down but he refused, standing beside me for seven hours. I was fortunate in having a relatively easy labour.

I gave one last push and the midwife lifted a tiny baby into my line of sight. 'You've got a little girl.' The baby let out a cry – she certainly had a set of lungs on her! – and the midwife placed her on my chest. I stared at the tiny, wriggling person. She had a shock of dark her like her father and was, quite simply, the most beautiful thing I'd ever seen.

She was taken away to be cleaned up and brought back to us wrapped in a pink blanket. The nurse placed her in Stephen's arms and his tears brimmed over. 'Hello, Lydia,' he said.

I looked up at him and smiled. It was a beautiful name for our girl. But where had it come from? It was an old name that one didn't hear too often. My face must have betrayed my quizzical thoughts for Stephen explained, 'I want our daughter to have a name like yours because I want her to be like you. Linda is close to Lydia but she will have her own name.' We gave her the middle name Susannah, after Stephen's maternal grandmother, which incorporated Ann in honour of beloved Aunty Ann.

Well, after the eight hours I'd just had, Stephen's lovely words tipped me over the edge. I began to cry tears of joy.

Later, when visiting hours began, two familiar figures arrived at my bedside. Mum, hair perfectly coiffed and clothes immaculately ironed, kissed my head and went straight to the cot beside me. As she cooed over Lydia, Dad – or should I say a walking bunch of flowers with arms and legs sticking out? – presented me with a huge bouquet of red roses. They both looked so proud.

Dad shook Stephen's hand. 'Congratulations, son.' Then, with a wink to me, he put his hand on Stephen's shoulder and said, 'How are you holding up?'

Stephen laughed. 'I've heard many say watching a child being born is a wonderful experience. But what's nice about seeing your wife in pain?'

'Well,' Mum said, Lydia cradled in the crook of her arm, 'forget about that. What might we be calling this beautiful little girl?'

We told them.

Dad beamed.

Mum frowned. 'You can't possibly call her Lydia,' she said. 'That's a terrible name. They'll be calling her Lid at school. Bin-lid!'

Dad took the baby in his arms and kissed her head. 'I think it's beautiful.'

After they'd left and Stephen went home to get showered and changed, I pulled the curtains around my bed and wept.

A voice called from the next bed, 'Are you all right?'

I pulled the curtain back and explained to Diana, a new mum like me, that Mum hated the name Stephen and I had chosen for our baby. She reached for my hand. 'Your Stephen is so lovely. My husband would never think of a romantic thing like naming our baby after me so she would be like me.'

Well, she was right. It was terribly romantic. And as Stephen had told me many times, 'You do like a bit of romance, dearest.'

I certainly did.

Diana continued, 'As soon as the registrar comes in I'll grab him and say, "Whatever Mrs Steliou says, her baby's called Lydia."'

That made me chuckle.

Later Stephen returned with a little black box much like the one he'd given to me on the eve of our wedding. I opened it and my hand fluttered to my chest. In the box I'd found a delicate gold chain and at the end of it a gold stork holding a baby. 'Thank you for giving me a beautiful daughter,' he murmured.

I pulled him close to me and kissed him.

In that moment, I realized that what Stephen and I wanted for our daughter was more important than any outside opinion, my mum's or otherwise.

When the registrar arrived, Diana didn't have to say a word. Stephen and I registered our daughter, who weighed six pounds ten ounces, as Lydia Susannah Steliou.

Next day, Dad returned with even more roses. He placed them around the statue of St Teresa in the lobby to thank the nurses for taking such good care of me and Lydia.

After visiting hours, when most of the ward mums were settling for the night with their babies, the nurses asked me to help them with something. I followed them into a side room, where a young Irish girl, no older than seventeen, lay with her baby boy in her arms. She looked so terribly sad and my heart went out to her. The nurses left me with Tina. We began to talk and I learned that Tina was from a staunch Catholic family. They had no idea she had been pregnant, and now did not know she'd given birth to a beautiful little boy, Liam. 'If my father finds out, he'll kill me,' she said. 'I have no choice but to give Liam away.'

A shiver ran through me. How sad it was that such a young girl was facing such a terrible dilemma, having to choose between her life, her family and her baby. It was impossible, surely, to take one of those options over another. I tried to persuade her to keep him, even offering my friendship and support, no matter what happened. But it was to no avail. Tina was terrified for her life.

I stayed with her for some time, listening to her stories and her reasoning. Eventually I returned to my bed, passing the nurses' station. They looked at me hopefully. I shook my head.

Next day, Tina and Liam were discharged from St Teresa's. I knew without doubt that mother and son had not left together. I held Lydia close and breathed in her scent. I had never felt so grateful for the support of my husband and parents.

I would have loved to keep in touch with Tina but, feeling sure she would think about her baby son every day, I didn't want to be a permanent reminder to her. I can but hope that life has turned out kinder for mother and son and that, if it hasn't done so already, Fate will bring them together again.

Lydia comes Home

Days later, we brought Lydia home and I couldn't wait to show her off. She wore pretty little dresses and a beautiful shawl, which Aunty Marie had crocheted. Lydia was my pride and joy. Stephen had returned to work and Mum popped in daily. She was fussing over Lydia when there was a knock at the door. Mum answered and returned seconds later with that look. 'It's your neighbour, Betty. She wants to see the baby.'

I didn't understand the delay. 'Mum, let her in!'

She didn't budge. 'She doesn't care about the baby, Linda,' she said. 'She just wants to get in here and see what you have and haven't got.'

Before I had a chance to answer, Betty had come through the open front door and was in the lounge with us. She rushed towards me, but instead of making for Lydia, she moved past us and placed her hand on the wall. 'Is that real pine cladding? Oh, it's lovely!' She looked up at the lights and then at our autumnal carpet, continuing to comment.

Mum stood behind her, arms crossed tightly and eyebrows raised. Her face was a picture. Then she said, in a tone which thoroughly matched that look, 'Betty, I thought you'd come to see the baby!'

Betty flushed and flew over to me, taking Lydia in

her arms and admiring her pretty pink dress. This time, I had to admit defeat. Mum had been spot on.

Soon enough, Stephen, Lydia and I found our own Steliou rhythm. If Lydia woke in the night, Stephen slipped out of bed, fetched her and placed her beside me in bed. He'd whisper, 'Dearest, please be careful. I've laid the baby by you while I fetch the bottle.' Minutes later he'd be back and, taking turns, we'd feed our little girl. I couldn't remember a time I'd ever been so happy. In the morning, he was up and away to work before Lydia or I had stirred.

We'd spend the day, mother and daughter, peacefully together. Though she was just a new-born baby, we had our own language. I soon understood what her cries meant and, really, she was such a good little girl. I adored her and being a mum. It felt natural for me to take care of another life and I wondered if, all these years, I'd been subconsciously preparing for it. Every day at five o'clock, I'd place Lydia in her pram and take her to wait for her daddy to return home from work. Our house was only a few yards from where our road joined the main bypass, along which he would come. I would sit on a bench, which was on a wide stretch of grass between the last house and the pavement, gently rocking Lydia's pram, in which she was cosily wrapped up against the chilly winter weather. As I waited, I looked at the nearby bus stop where I had first met Win and smiled as I recalled how much she had helped me on the bus that day.

I would have loved to bring home a puppy, which

would compel me to go out for walks, but it wasn't possible for the time being. Nevertheless I sent up a silent prayer that I would be freed from those awful panic attacks, for the sake of my husband and our baby daughter as well as myself.

One day I was listening to a local radio show when a Dr Julian Harper came on to talk about phobias. To start with, there wasn't anything I hadn't heard before, but then he said something that made me sit up and listen: 'When you have a phobia, often your partner suffers with you because their life becomes restricted too.'

I thought about Stephen and tears filled my eyes. I *was* restricting his life. We didn't go on holidays or leave Raynes Park. We hadn't even had a honeymoon. Though Stephen had been nothing but understanding and compassionate, I knew it wasn't fair on him. I had to do something about my panic attacks. Stephen made me an appointment at Kingston Hospital with Dr Harper and we went along together.

Dr Harper said, 'Stephen, what are your thoughts on Linda's panic attacks?'

Stephen explained that we'd been together since I was fifteen. He'd seen the attacks develop and he felt so sorry for me because their severity prevented me living life to the full, and he didn't know how to help me get better.

I squeezed his hand.

But his words made me think. I hadn't been born having panic attacks: they had indeed developed.

Before they'd started, I'd been an adventurer, taking school trips to Lake Como, Italy, and later St Moritz in Switzerland. I hadn't been in the slightest concerned about how we'd arrived at our destination.

Stephen continued, 'I don't know exactly how it feels to be gripped by a panic attack because I've never experienced one, but I do know this for certain: Linda suffers.'

'Do the pair of you realize that when one suffers, the other's life is limited?' Dr Harper added, as he had on the radio, 'And because of that, the couple are often driven apart.'

While I could understand that, the mere thought of not having Stephen in my life was unbearable. There and then I made a silent vow to him that I would do all I could to get better.

Every day, I placed Lydia in her pram and took her for a walk. At first, I'd go to the end of our road, turn left and head for the butcher. If there was more than one customer waiting, the panic would rise in my chest and I'd virtually run with the pram till I was once more in the safety of our lovely home. But every day I pushed myself a bit more, and every day, we went a bit further. Gradually, I was able to take Lydia to the park, a twenty-minute walk away. It wasn't without difficulty on my part but I loved putting Lydia in the swing and seeing her smile. I took her on the roundabout and held her tightly in my arms as we spun, like Dad had done with me on the helter-skelter all those years ago.

Mum was over-protective of Lydia and fiercely proud. Dad was softer, fun-loving and always full of the joys of spring. One afternoon, while Lydia slept, I was talking to Aunty Ann and we were trying to figure out what had triggered my panics. Aunty Ann told me that when I'd been a little girl, Mum had taken me every Saturday to visit her brother and his wife. We'd get a bus to Morden, then hop on the Tube from Morden to Borough. But instead of holding me on her lap or leaving me in my pram, she'd remove my nappy and sit me on a potty with a blanket across my lap. As a mother now, I was shocked by the notion. 'Why would Mum do that?' I asked, perplexed.

Aunty Ann said, 'Your mum didn't want you to be uncomfortable.'

Could that long-forgotten embarrassment somehow have found its way to my stomach upsets as a young adult, resulting in the panic attacks? Whatever the answer, when Mum told me that she wanted to put Lydia on a potty when she took her on a train, as she had done with me, I refused. 'That's ridiculous, Mum. She'll be fine in her nappy.'

She raised her eyebrows. 'You don't care about that baby. If you did, you'd want to make sure she was always comfortable!'

Her hurtful comment upset me. On the contrary, it was because I *did* care, and care deeply, about Lydia that I wanted to do my utmost to ensure that she would never suffer from panic attacks as I did. It made sense to me that my mum's over-protectiveness in my

Driving Lessons

When Lydia was two, Stephen encouraged me to have driving lessons. He thought if I was in control of how I was travelling, it would ease my anxiety, and found a sympathetic instructor to guide me through the process. By then, I needed to stay within a two-mile radius of my home, but the instructor understood and adapted his routes to stick close to that area. Over time, though, we went a little further until there were days when I did not recognize the roads we were on.

I sat my driving test and passed first time!

On my first drive with Lydia in the car, I talked to her until she was fast asleep. It hadn't been until I'd glanced in the rear-view mirror and seen her head against the side of her little seat and her eyes firmly shut that I'd realized she was snoozing. In that moment, I felt as if I'd been sucked into a time machine: I wasn't a twenty-five-year-old driving her sleeping child home, I was seven years old, peering through the fence at a little dog that had fallen asleep in a flowerbed while I'd talked his ear off. 'Oh, Teddy,' I said now, 'my for-ever friend. I miss you even to this day.'

There was something else my new-found freedom meant, which affected not only me but Stephen and Lydia too. Together Stephen and I drove to Morden and, by appointment, we viewed a house. It was a terraced property with three bedrooms and a long back garden. It was a few minutes' drive from Mum and Dad and, although in need of total refurbishment, it was ours.

Yet again, Stephen had his work on our new home well cut out for him. In spite of working long hours at his job, he devoted all his evenings and weekends to DIY.

One day shortly after we had moved in, I was clipping the unruly hedge in the front garden when an elderly neighbour came across the road. 'I want to welcome you but also to say, please don't think we're all like the people from whom you bought this house! We couldn't believe our eyes when we saw them digging up all the lovely plants and shrubs and taking them away with them before you moved in.'

Indeed, they hadn't only removed those from the front garden, they'd taken every single plant and shrub from the hundred-and-twenty-foot back garden, leaving only one tree, which was no doubt too difficult to dig up – and the unmown lawn! I thanked the lady for her concern, adding, with a smile, 'It's a pity they didn't take this hedge too!'

Klerry Annette

During my pregnancy with Lydia, one of the medical secretaries, Vivienne, with whom I'd worked at Nelson Hospital told me about her three-year-old daughter, Laura.

Coincidentally, Vivienne's blood group was the same as mine, O Rhesus negative, and her husband's was the same as Stephen's, O Rhesus positive. She added that, at her post-natal examination, she had been advised to leave a gap of five years before she had another baby: any children they had together might inherit his blood group, which would clash with hers, thereby endangering the unborn baby. At my post-natal examination, I told the obstetrician what Vivienne had said, and she confirmed that it was, indeed, advisable to wait that long before trying for another child. We had hoped to give Lydia a baby sister or brother after a couple of years but, following doctor's orders, we erred, as we thought, on the side of safety.

However, because it had taken a long while for me to conceive Lydia, we decided not to wait the complete five years before we tried for another baby. This time I became pregnant quickly. When I received a card from the hospital telling me to attend urgently, Stephen and I were sick with worry. I broke down in front of the obstetrician. 'We should have waited the whole five years,' I sobbed.

'What do you mean?' he asked.

I told him about Vivienne, that she and I had been advised to leave a five-year gap. He looked at me kindly. 'I'm sorry, Mrs Steliou, but there was some misunderstanding on the part of the obstetrician. It's advisable for any new mother to wait for about a year before embarking on another pregnancy, simply to allow time for her body to settle down. In your case, your baby may have a different blood group from you, which can cause problems, regardless of how long you wait between babies. I'm afraid that both you and your friend need not have waited so long.'

I could hardly believe that both Vivienne and I had been misinformed by obstetricians.

Our happiness at my expecting our second baby was overshadowed with worry, because of any risk to our baby. And in spite of my expanding girth I never felt the slightest movement. During my first pregnancy, I'd felt flutterings at around four months and, from then on, Lydia had moved around like a footballer. Seven months into my second pregnancy, I was sent for an ultrasound scan. It didn't help matters when the sonographer, moving the instrument across my abdomen, commented, 'I can't find any heartbeat.' Fearing the worst, I began to cry – until suddenly she paused, pressed the instrument into the lower left-hand side of my abdomen and we heard, 'Beep-beep, beep-beep . . .'

'That's your baby's heartbeat!' she said. My tears of sorrow turned into sobs of relief and joy.

Two weeks later, I felt the baby move for the first time.

The birth was induced at thirty-eight weeks, which couldn't come soon enough. As soon as our baby was born, she was whisked away to the special-care baby unit.

Stephen and Lydia were waiting outside the delivery room, with a huge bouquet. I'd so wanted to be the one to tell them about our baby, but one of the midwives had beaten me to it. I was wheeled to the ward, with Stephen and Lydia hurrying alongside the trolley. Stephen was as anxious as I was to see our new daughter, as was Lydia, who had 'ordered' a baby sister! I was told that, because I had had an epidural, I would have to wait for the effects to wear off before I saw her but I was determined to go there and then. Stephen pushed me in a wheelchair, with Lydia trotting excitedly beside us.

On our arrival, a nurse pointed out where Baby Steliou was sleeping in an incubator. 'You wanted a baby sister, Lydia, and here she is,' I said.

Lydia's face crumpled. 'But I don't want that one!' The poor little mite looked more like an Outspan orange than a new baby. The nurse tried to reassure us by saying that she looked that colour because of the lighting, but the skin of the baby in the next incubator, under the same light, was the normal shade of pink. Our baby had to have frequent blood tests. I couldn't bear to hear her cry out when the haematologist needed to pinch her tiny heel to take the blood. 'If Baby Steliou has to have all her blood changed, I want her mother a million miles away from here,' he said. Thank God (and, believe me, we did), she didn't need to have that done.

We named her Klerry Annette. I'd always liked the name Kerry, and Klerry was Stephen's paternal grand-mother's name, so that pleased her greatly. Annette is in honour of my beloved Aunty Ann. It's French, meaning 'Little Ann' and, indeed, Aunty Ann was little – little in height but huge in heart!

Bringing Klerry Home

We soon settled into our new house with our new baby. Mum and Dad popped in as often as they could and I revelled in being mum to two little girls. Everywhere I took them, people stopped to comment on how pretty they were. My mind flew back to the twin dolls of my childhood. Lydia and Klerry's curly brown hair, lovely eyes and rosebud lips were their mirror image, but with the added advantage of being 'the real thing'. I had fulfilled my mother-in-law's wish for a grand-daughter not once but twice. Plus, Lydia was the mirror image of Stephen who, in turn, was very like his mother. Klerry also took after her dad's side of the family, being like her uncle Michael, Stephen's youngest brother. Character-wise, Lydia, as a child, was also like her dad: she was quite serious and very academic. Klerry reminded me more of her maternal granddad, William, and Aunty Ann.

When Klerry was three months old, I found Lydia sitting at the bottom of the stairs before school. She told me her tummy was hurting and big tears rolled down her face. I didn't waste any time. I took her straight to the surgery at the corner of our road. There, the GP examined Lydia as I held Klerry. She was due for a feed and was fidgety.

The doctor sighed. 'I think this episode is because you have a new baby in the house and Lydia is hoping for a bit of attention.'

I looked at my elder daughter, her eyes red from crying. 'Thank you, Doctor.' I left the clinic, rang Stephen and asked him to come home. When he arrived, I took Lydia straight to hospital. She was not a child to seek attention. If she told me she was in pain, she was.

No sooner had she been examined than the doctor in Casualty admitted her and sent her up to the surgical team. She had peritonitis. As she was rushed to the operating theatre, I sank into a chair in the family room and put my head in my hands. Thank God I'd ignored that first doctor.

Hours later, my daughter was brought back to the children's ward. She was groggy from the anaesthetic and her little face was pale. I felt a mix of worry and rage at the doctor's wrong diagnosis. But as I held Lydia's little hand, she gave mine a squeeze, and I knew she was going to be fine. I sat by her side, stroking her face and hair, telling her how much I loved her, when I heard Charlie Rich singing 'The Most Beautiful Girl' across the hall. Earlier, it was Lydia whose face had been wet with tears. Now, it was me who was crying.

Lydia remained in hospital for a few days and, with Klerry well looked after at home, I slept beside her bed until she was discharged, just a few days before my birthday. Her recovery was the best gift I could have wished for. The moment we brought her home, something magical happened. When Klerry saw her sister, she giggled. The sound made us all stop in our tracks. When Klerry was born, the nurse who took her away to be weighed and monitored said she was certain she'd seen the baby smile. Everyone had heard Granddad Peck's story of how Dad had come into the world with a smile on his face. I'd always wondered if it was true or if Granddad had imagined it later because Dad was always smiling. After I'd heard the nurse's story about Klerry, I reckoned Granddad had been right all along.

Soon, Lydia went back to school, and Klerry grew fast. I'd barely blinked before she was talking and walking. At weekends, Mum loved to take the girls shopping. She spoiled them just as she'd spoiled me, but one day when she'd got back and the girls had gone off to play, she said, 'You know what, Linda? I've never seen girls like your two.'

'What do you mean?' I said.

'Do you know how many times I've taken the girls into a shop for toys or sweets and told them I'd like to treat them, only to be refused?'

'What do you mean, Mum?'

'They always say, "Thank you, Nan, but we have everything we want."'

I was pleased that they were well-mannered, just as I was pleased that, for once, I had finally done something right in my mum's eyes.

Back to Work

After I became pregnant with Klerry, an orthopaedic surgeon, for whom I'd worked at Nelson Hospital, contacted me to ask if I would be interested in typing his letters from my home. I was more than delighted to. He and I had always got on well and it would be lovely to see him again. Plus, his work was interesting and it would help me keep my typing speed up. I always kept up my shorthand by taking down news items from the television, or words from songs that were playing, and would also write my shopping lists in shorthand.

Every week the consultant came to my home to deliver his tapes and notes, and collect the letters and medical reports I had typed for him. It should have been a two-minute visit, but each day, without fail, he'd let out a big sigh, rub his forehead and wait for me to ask, 'Do you have time for a quick coffee?'

He'd grin. 'For you, Linda, always.'

We both knew that, although his schedule was jam-packed as he rushed from one hospital to the next, then into the theatre for surgery, he was glad of a quick breather. We had more in common than our love of all things medical. He, too, had a daughter, Katie, who was four years younger than Lydia. When I gave birth to Klerry, he would bring me beautiful clothes that

Katie had outgrown. Although Klerry had plenty of lovely dresses, she didn't have anything from the renowned department store Harrods, where Katie's dresses had been bought.

Like me, the surgeon was a dog lover. In fact, he had four dogs, which he enjoyed talking about. In turn, I regaled him with stories about my adventures with Teddy and how one day, when I had the time and space to take a puppy into our home, I would have one of my own.

In time, he and his wife invited Stephen and me for dinner at their home.

Luckily, it was within my two-mile safety zone. As we arrived at their door, there was a cacophony of barking, as the dogs warned of unknown intruders at the door. It showed why dogs are such an excellent deterrent to any would-be burglar. As the door opened and we stepped inside, the barking quietened and the dogs wagged their tails as they gathered around us, weaving in and out of our legs, sniffing me, then Stephen.

For some first-time unsuspecting visitors it would have been a relief to know they were not on the menu that night for a dog's dinner. For me, though, being around those gorgeous dogs and feeling their warmth brought back a familiar longing. I had either suppressed it or had been so busy with the girls that I'd all but forgotten my unfulfilled childhood dream. Would I ever have a dog to call my own?

Stephen and I had discussed it many times, but with the girls, work and little Leo to contend with, we didn't have the time to spare that a family dog would deserve. As ever, my dream was shelved. But as Fate, or luck, would have it, an opportunity soon presented itself to give me a daily dose of puppy love.

Dr R. I. L. ('Jock') Smallwood

It was September 1976 when an advertisement appeared in the local newspaper for a medical secretary, working for a private general practitioner in Wimbledon. As happy as I was to be a wife and a mother, the panic attacks from which I suffered stopped me enjoying life to the full.

Now, with the job advert in my hands, I sat down with a cup of coffee and mulled over applying for the post. I knew I would love the job but the journey to and from work would involve a bus, if not a car journey, in rush-hour. Could I handle it? By the time I'd finished my coffee, I'd made my decision. I couldn't let anxiety and panic attacks confine me for ever. I picked up the telephone and dialled the number on the advert. No sooner had it started ringing than it was answered. 'Dr Smallwood,' said a voice.

My goodness, I thought. If only all surgeries answered the telephone so quickly! I introduced myself and told Dr Smallwood that I was phoning regarding the vacancy for a medical secretary.

He had a lovely soothing voice and a pleasant manner. He sounded pleased to hear from me and I wondered why he was without a secretary. Perhaps he'd had one who had left because she was moving away or about to embark on motherhood. Whatever the reason, I was sure it would have had nothing to do with Dr Smallwood. I gave him a brief outline of my experience as a medical secretary. He listened carefully, then said, 'I'd like you to come and see me for a face-to-face interview as soon as possible.'

Next day, a friend kindly gave me a lift to the interview.

We pulled up outside Dr Smallwood's house and she wished me the best of luck. I took a deep breath, stepped out of the car and made my way up the garden path. The house was very like a country cottage, with creeping ivy on the walls and glorious flowers growing wildly in the garden. The door was painted white with a big black lion's head knocker. I'd hardly had time to knock before the door was opened – he must have been waiting for me in the hall. He greeted me with a warm smile – and the minute I clocked his twinkling blue eyes, I realized I'd met him when I was a child and he'd covered for our usual GP, Dr Metcalf.

Dr Smallwood invited me in, and as I stepped inside, a white flash raced towards me.

The gorgeous little dog, a West Highland White Terrier, stopped by Dr Smallwood, mostly ignoring me, and trotted happily at his master's side as we walked along the hallway. Eventually we went into the surgery, which was attached to the side of the house.

'Now, Skip,' Dr Smallwood began, focusing on the dog at his feet, 'you know this area is out of bounds for you, so be a good boy and wait for me in your basket. I won't be long.'

Skip looked up at him, tilting his head to one side, as clever dogs do when paying attention to what is being said to them. Then, his eyes met mine, and seemed to say, 'It was nice to have met you. Perhaps we can have a chat and a cuddle later on.' With that, he turned tail and trotted off to wait patiently in his basket.

In that moment, I knew I was the woman for the most perfect job.

The door at the end of the hall led into the surgery's office, from which another door opened into the consulting room. We went into the office and Dr Smallwood invited me to take a seat. I did so and said, 'We've met before, Dr Smallwood.'

He looked at me as quizzically as Skip had.

'With the number of patients you must have seen over the years, I doubt very much that you'll remember me,' I went on, 'especially as I was only a young child at the time. However, to my eyes, you look just as you did then.'

Twenty-five years had passed, and although his hair had greyed and there were more crinkles around his eyes, Dr Smallwood was much the same.

'Really?' he asked.

'Really,' I replied, then reminded him that once, when Dr Metcalf had been away on holiday, he had been Dr Metcalf's junior partner and had treated my cough and cold.

He chuckled and the knot of anxiety in my chest disappeared.

Just as his kindly manner had put me at ease all those years earlier when I had been his patient, it did so now when I hoped to become his secretary.

Dr Smallwood explained that the lady who had been his secretary for many years had retired and was moving miles away, hence his need for someone to replace her.

I gave him a more detailed account of my experience as a medical secretary in various departments at Nelson Hospital, and he smiled when I mentioned consultants for whom I had worked and to whom he had referred patients. I had been even typed replies and reports from those consultants to him.

As the interview drew to a close and I wondered whether or not my application had been successful, Dr Smallwood opened a drawer in his desk. He pulled out a small pile of letters and handed them to me. 'Linda, I'd like to offer you the post, and if you wish to accept, your first task will be to answer these.'

Even if I was talking with my eyes, I wanted to make absolutely sure that Dr Smallwood knew how delighted I was to be offered the job. I thanked him, then added, 'I'm delighted, and can't wait to get started.'

My friend had taken herself off while I was having my interview, for a look round the shops, so I told Dr Smallwood that, if it was convenient to him, I could deal with the letters while I was waiting for her to return. He had finished his morning surgery and was about to go out on house calls but said that, by all means, I could answer the letters and leave them ready for him to sign when he returned. We shook hands and he left the room. I heard Skip's bark of a greeting as Dr Smallwood went to him.

As I set about my first task as his secretary, I discovered that all of the letters he had handed to me were in response to his advertisement. Some applicants had written about their secretarial background, but none had any knowledge of medical terminology. Others, though, had sent very good CVs, which showed plenty of appropriate experience. I was pleased that I'd taken the bull by the horns and telephoned instead of writing. Otherwise, another young woman might have been sitting in that office chair, with me on the receiving end of the letter I was about to type, thanking each for their interest while informing them – to my glee – that the post had been filled.

When I had finished, I put the envelopes containing the rejection letters in a neat little pile on the desk, ready for Dr Smallwood to sign. I also left a handwritten note thanking him again for giving me this marvellous opportunity, for which I was more than grateful.

If I had known then that this would be the start of the happiest eighteen years of my working life, I would have had an even bigger smile on my face.

As I closed the main surgery door behind me and heard it lock automatically, my friend's car was pulling up outside. I opened the passenger door to climb in beside her. 'You must be psychic,' I said. 'Your timing's perfect.'

'And if your grin is anything to go by, you must be Dr Smallwood's new secretary.'

Indeed I was!

My next-door neighbour, Diane, had two boys, Ian, who was fifteen months older than Klerry, and Darren, eight months younger. She was happy to take care of Klerry for a few hours every day, so in the morning, I would take Klerry to Diane's, Lydia to school, and look forward to being greeted by Skip. I felt a lovely sense of freedom at being able to get back into the world, even if mine was not as big and wide as I wished it was.

First Day on the Job

It wasn't long before I was outside Dr Smallwood's charming house again. My mind was drawn back to another doctor's surgery I had attended a quarter of a century earlier. While the stark black and white paint-work on its exterior walls might have been fashionable at the time, to a young child – me – who was already nervous at the prospect of a dreaded injection, it looked like the house of doom. I was sure no child would feel so apprehensive on approaching Dr Smallwood's surgery.

I opened the door to the surgery and walked to my desk, which was in the office between the waiting room and the consulting room, wondering who would be the first patient I'd meet that day. Dr Smallwood was already in his consulting room, his door wide open. When he saw me, he stood up and greeted me with a smile. He complimented me on the letters I'd typed on the day of my interview, then held open the door that led from my office into the main house.

I was standing in the hallway when Skip padded towards us. I bent down to stroke him, his little tail wagging like a flag being waved in welcome. Dr Small-wood smiled. 'I think he's taken to you already.'

'Well, the feeling's mutual,' I replied.

I was shown into the first room off to the right, a neat kitchen, and told to help myself to tea and coffee whenever I liked. The second room on the right was the cloakroom, so I took off my coat, hung it on the peg, and went back into my office. My office! I was at work, but already I felt totally at home. There was about twenty minutes or so until the first patient was due. I sat on my chair, adjusted the back and pulled the cover off the typewriter, ready to get to grips with whatever the day threw at me.

Dr Smallwood appeared in the doorway, holding two cups of coffee. He handed me one. 'I thought you might enjoy a cup now, while we go through a few points about the practice.'

I learned that the patients' notes were kept in alphabetical order on a large, cylindrical rotating filing system in the corner of the office. From my desk drawer, Dr Smallwood produced the account ledgers and placed them to one side of the typewriter and the appointments diary on the other. At my interview, he had said that part of my work would consist of sending out the accounts monthly. I had confessed that maths had not been my strong point at school, but he'd reassured me that the accounts would be straightforward and he would show me how to do them. Now, as he demonstrated, I sighed with relief.

Throughout the morning, as each patient turned up for their appointment, Dr Smallwood would come out of his consulting room to introduce me to them. This went on all day. Most wished me luck in my new job, but no one needed to: I felt like the luckiest employee in the world for having the opportunity to work with Dr Smallwood.

And my already good luck was about to get even better. My husband bought me a car. I had no idea that I would be in for such a fantastic surprise, and it enabled me to have control over my journey to and from work – it was a godsend.

While Dr Smallwood was consulting, I busied myself with getting a feel for the work I would be doing. On reading back through the appointments diary, I saw that the names of certain patients cropped up regularly and they needed quite lengthy appointments. There was no such thing as a definitive ten-minute consultation and I soon learned that all of Dr Smallwood's patients were given the amount of time they needed with him. No one would ever have felt they were being rushed out of his surgery. I made up my mind that I, too, would be as accommodating, helpful and kind as I could to the patients. No way would any of them ever have cause to categorize me as one of those receptionists you couldn't get past to see or speak to the doctor. In all my forty years as a medical secretary, I stuck to that resolution. Also, whatever concerns I had in my personal life, and there were plenty over the years, I never allowed them to affect my work. I took a leaf out of Dad's book: I kept a smile on my face and always did my best.

By now, I was thirty-one, Lydia eight and Klerry two and a half. When I wasn't working, we had lots of fun together. One evening, I was getting Klerry ready to pick up Lydia from Brownies when she held up her finger. 'One minute, Mummy.' She raced upstairs and when she came back down, a giggle burst out of her. I stared at her, then laughed.

Klerry had fetched her shampoo halo, a yellow three-inch-deep plastic fringe that I clipped around her forehead and under her hair to stop the suds getting into her eyes.

'What have you got that on for, you silly sausage?' I said. 'We're going out now!'

But Klerry was adamant. 'I want to wear my hat,' she insisted.

Well, who was I to stop her?

In the pushchair she was wearing a pretty pink and white dress, frilly socks, pink shoes, and that ridiculous plastic halo. All the way to the Brownie hut, people smiled at me and laughed at Klerry's outfit. Klerry laughed along with them.

Somehow my shifts with Dr Smallwood, family life and time with Stephen worked in harmony. In time, Klerry went to Lydia's old school, where she was joined by Diane's boys.

One morning, I took a day's holiday so that I could attend a school dance production.

Klerry, seven, was partnered with Diane's son Ian, eight. Like his parents, Ian was very tall.

In fact, when he was born and Diane came home with him, we'd been chatting over the garden fence when she'd passed him to me for a cuddle. He seemed almost the length of one of the fencing panels! Now he was literally twice Klerry's height.

Mum and I sat in the audience as the children began to sing and dance. Ian swung Klerry round, and with every spin her feet lifted clear off the ground. As her bunches flew out, I laughed. What a sight! Mum was frowning. She hated bunches.

When Father Christmas
came to Morden

At infant school, Klerry made friends easily and among them were Siu-Fong, six, and her younger brother, Chung Man, Klerry's age. Their parents, May-Ling and Ma-Ong, owned a local fish-and-chip shop. One day, when I popped in to buy some, May-Ling, with her usual sweet smile, greeted me, then said, 'Please, may I ask you a favour, Linda?'

'Of course,' I replied.

May-Ling explained that although they had been living in England for ten years, she had not had an opportunity to make any friends: her life revolved around working long hours in the business and taking care of the children and her mother-in-law. 'As your daughter, Klerry, is such a good friend to my children, it would make me very happy if you would be my friend, Linda.'

Bless her heart. 'It would be my pleasure,' I told her.

We gave each other a hug and, from that day forth, we were firm friends.

That Christmas, I invited Siu-Fong and Chung-Man to tea with Klerry. May-Ling was too busy to come with them. The children went into the living room while I set to work in the kitchen, preparing tea. After a while, I popped my head through the hatch to ask the children what they'd like to drink. At the far end of the living room I saw Siu-Fong holding her younger brother's hand. The pair of them were gazing up at all the shimmering Christmas chains and decorations, then at the sparkly Christmas tree. They were mesmerized.

I stopped what I was doing and joined them in the living room. 'Has Mummy put your Christmas tree and decorations up yet?'

When they looked a bit blank, I added, 'Father Christmas will be coming soon.'

Tears filled Chung Man's eyes. 'Father Christmas does not come to Hong Kong.'

Though we were very much in England, I understood what he meant.

Stephen walked through the door just in time to see me sweep the little boy into my arms and say, 'Well, Father Christmas does come to Morden!'

Stephen smiled, no doubt guessing what I had in mind.

I wanted to make sure that those children would have as happy a Christmas as I could make for them. Just weeks earlier, I had bought new decorations so the old ones were packed away in boxes but still lovely. I gathered them together and, when it was time for me to take Siu-Fong and Chung Man home, they couldn't wait to show May-Ling and Ma-Ong what I'd given them to decorate their home.

The parents thanked me and told the children they'd put the decorations up as soon as the shop quietened down. It was Saturday night, and if the shop, which was teeming with customers, was anything to go by, the Wongs had several hours' cooking ahead of them.

I had an idea, and when I put it to May-Ling and Ma-Ong, they were thanking me again.

I took their children to their flat above the shop and set up the Christmas decorations. Those children's faces lit up even more than my children's did – Lydia and Klerry were used to the festivities, no matter how much they enjoyed them. The entire family, plus Grandma, were thrilled with their Christmas wonderland.

It was only after the decorations were up and the children were in bed that May-Ling and I finally had a moment to sit down together. May-Ling told me again how grateful she was for what I had done – she had been upset to see her children sad after they'd discovered how exciting Christmas was from their friends at school.

Next day, I slipped on my Santa's Little Helper hat and set off to do some shopping. I bought Christmas stockings and sacks, then the presents with which to fill them. While Siu-Fong and Chung Man were out of the way at school, I took everything to May-Ling and Ma-Ong. 'I know how short of time you both are so I hope you don't mind that I took the liberty of doing a little shopping.'

Their thanks were nothing compared to the satisfaction I took from their delight. Then they thanked me again, several times. Finally, I said, 'Don't. The pleasure really was all mine. I'm only sorry that I can't be Father Christmas because I'd probably get stuck in the chimney!'

We all had a good laugh, and I went home, thinking, as Dad would say, If everyone's happy, I'm happy.

After Christmas, I went back to work with Dr Smallwood in his homely office.

I enjoyed working for him but there was one part of my day I especially loved. Whenever I left my desk and went into the kitchen for a cup of coffee, a little face would be waiting for me. I'd talk to Skip about my day and tell him my latest news. He waited patiently by my feet, waiting for a pat on the head or a rub of his belly. He was a lovely little dog and his temperament reminded me of Teddy. Sometimes, if I fell silent, Skip would look up at me and tilt his head, as if to say, 'Well? Go on, then.'

It took all the strength I had not to ask Dr Smallwood, affectionately known to his patients as Dr Jock, if I could take Skip for a walk. I might have been a married mother of two but my passion for dogs showed no sign of waning any time soon.

Dr Smallwood made his patients, young or old, feel so at ease that it seemed more as if they were visiting a much-loved grandfather than their doctor. As he had known most of the children since the day they had been born, and their parents before them, I wasn't surprised to learn that he was considered by many to be part of the family. I had settled in with him happily and, with Lydia and Klerry at school full-time, my working hours increased.

Dr Smallwood had a very busy practice and there was never a dull moment. I came to know his patients well, almost as though they were my extended family. Consequently, as one would with family, I shared their highs and lows, and often they popped in early for an appointment so that we could have a chat. The young engaged couples would keep me up to date with their plans for the forthcoming wedding. I loved hearing all the details!

Those who were already married and eagerly awaiting the birth of a child would chat to me about the names they had chosen. For fun, I used to do what became known as Linda's needle test: I would thread a needle and dangle it over the expectant mother's bump to find out the baby's sex. I had started doing this when I was the maternity secretary at the Nelson Hospital. About 80 per cent of those over whom the needle swung in a circle had a baby boy, and practically every single one over whom the needle swung in a straight line delivered a girl.

When I was pregnant with Klerry, I carried out my needle test on a group of fourteen women, of whom twelve, including me, delivered the sex predicted. One of the women over whom the needle had swung in a circle, exclaimed, 'Oh, no! I already have two boys and I'd love to have a little girl.'

'Perhaps yours will be in the twenty per cent that weren't boys when the needle swung in a circle,' I said consolingly.

Several weeks later, I was out shopping when I happened to bump into the woman. She told me that of those fourteen women who had had their babies, my needle test had proved accurate. 'I'm now convinced that I'm having a third boy,' she said. And, a couple of weeks later, she did!

Another needle-test situation arose when an old school friend of mine, Margaret, who already had six children, was pregnant again. The needle didn't just swing in a straight line, it whizzed back and forth so fast that I wondered aloud if it might indicate twin girls. We both laughed.

A few months later, I was woken by the telephone ringing. I switched on the bedside lamp and glanced at the clock next to it. It was eleven thirty at night, and as people usually call late when something is amiss, I practically fell out of the bed and flew down the stairs. In the hall I grabbed the receiver, and my anxiety must have shown in my voice because the caller laughed. 'Don't sound so worried. Everything's fine!'

It was Margaret. Still half asleep, my thoughts went rapidly into overdrive. Was she in labour? Hopefully not, as the baby wasn't due for another month. If she was, did she need me to drive her to the hospital? That didn't make sense either: she lived almost opposite the hospital and would get there quicker on foot than if I drove from Morden to Roehampton to take her.

'I'm sorry to ring so late, Linda, especially if I got you worried, but I just had to let you know that I've had them!'

'Them?' I was starting to wake up. 'You haven't had twins, have you?'

'No, not twins ... I've had *triplets* and they're all girls!'

Well, I was definitely wide awake now. No wonder that needle had been whizzing! We both had a good old laugh and a chat about the new additions.

Margaret said Cliff, her husband, had named the first two Nicola and Denise but now they'd run out of names – they'd already had four daughters, as well as two sons. 'So we'd like you to christen the third,' she finished.

I felt very honoured and suggested 'Kerry' as the baby's name.

As Margaret settled down for some well-deserved, much-needed sleep, I climbed back up the stairs to bed. When I came into the bedroom Stephen stirred. 'Is everything all right?' Still in a state of shock, I told him, 'Margaret's had triplets!'

'Well, it's nothing to do with me,' he responded sleepily.

'I should hope not!' I replied, laughing.

A second or two later, he sat bolt upright. 'Did you just say that Margaret's had triplets?'

'She certainly has!'

The next day, I went to visit the newcomers, and as I entered the ward, Paul, their elder brother, ran to me. 'Aunty Linda, Mum's had triplets! We were going to go on a holiday this year but now Mum and Dad can't afford to go. But we don't care! Anyone can go on holiday, but not everyone has triplets!'

How lovely, I thought, putting an arm around him and letting the proud brother lead the way to his new little sisters.

Moving Office

For as long as I'd known Dr Smallwood, it had been his dream to open a private hospital near Wimbledon Common. Eventually, he did so, with the help of two of his patients, both civil engineers. On top of his general practice, he was now its medical director. I joined him there to take up my new position as general medical secretary. As much as I had loved working from Dr Smallwood's home, I liked the change of scene. The hospital was surrounded by magnificent grounds, tended by Peter, the gardener. To my delight, Peter had a brown and white Springer Spaniel, which came with him to work.

The very first time I saw Bramble, I wanted to make a fuss of her. Soon she began to trot along behind me to my office, which was based in what used to be a cottage, beyond the car park at the far end of the hospital grounds. As she nipped at my heels and raced around me, a voice called, 'Stay, Bramble!'

Perhaps Peter thought she was making a nuisance of herself. When he came to greet me, I set him straight. I'd always wanted a dog of my own and had never had one, so I'd enjoy Bramble's company. Every day, Bramble would be waiting to greet me when I pulled up in my car for work. She seemed to know instinctively what time I would arrive and where I would park, and would be waiting on the same spot for me, day after day. As I drove through the gates, she would get to her feet, tail wagging, and grin at me – at least, I liked to think she did. It was easy to translate her woofs. *I wonder what treats Linda has for me today.* And there I was, thinking she loved me for myself!

As soon as I'd parked, Bramble, unable to contain herself, would leap up at the driver's window, front paws hanging on to the framework, her nose pressed against the glass. *Well, hurry up, then, so that we can have our usual hug and my treat!* Needless to say, I was only too happy to oblige. I would have a couple of doggy treats in my palm and open the car door carefully so as not to hurt her. Initially, she would try to leap on to my lap but, as lovely as it would have been for me to sit there with her for a while, duty called.

She soon learned that if she sat down, like a good girl, and let me get out of the car, she would be rewarded with treats. Together, Bramble and I would make our way the short distance to the cottage where she would vie with me as to who would get through the door first to dash to a certain drawer in my desk, which did not contain the usual secretarial tools of the trade. She didn't care for shorthand pads, pens, pencils, medical dictionaries: it was the extra treats I'd stashed there for her.

She would stand on her back legs, nose and paws to the drawer, whining at my inability to run like she did through the cottage. Soon she had taken to sitting on the side wall between the hospital's main entrance and the car park so that she would see me and get at the treats that much quicker. I'd pull up, wind down the window, and Bramble would leap in, squashing herself between the steering-wheel and my chest, then smother my face with licks, while I tried to keep her wagging bottom from tooting the hooter. Every day, her shenanigans had me in stitches. It was a wonder I didn't crash the car.

One day, to my sorrow and, I believe, Bramble's, the news came that she and Peter were moving to Wales. I said a sorrowful goodbye to Bramble during my lunch break, walking through the hospital grounds and giving her treats. It was naughty of me to spoil her but it was the last time I'd see her. While my feet dragged with the knowledge she was leaving, Bramble was none the wiser, dashing back and forth with a present for me – a twig or a mouthful of whatever rubbish she'd found.

I knelt down and stroked her head, behind her ears and down her glossy back. 'I'll miss you, girl,' I said. But there was no time for nostalgia. She must have caught a whiff of something for she was off again. As we neared the cottage, I spotted Peter. I gave him a wave, having said goodbye earlier in the day, and went inside. I couldn't bear to say a proper goodbye to Bramble.

As much as I loved my work, I missed Bramble. But though she had gone from my working life, she never left my heart or thoughts.

Holidays with Nan and Granddad

While my working life was in full flow, I still hadn't managed to conquer my anxiety over travelling so, every year, Mum and Dad took the girls away. I was sad to be missing out on the girls' holidays, but at least my issues weren't holding them back. Besides, Mum and Dad loved having the girls to themselves for a fortnight, as much as Lydia and Klerry enjoyed being with them. Just as Mum and Dad had created so many lovely memories for me in Ramsgate, they were now doing the same for my daughters at Pontins. For that, I was eternally grateful. The girls would come home bubbling over with all the things they'd done and experienced.

When I asked what their favourite bit of the holiday had been, Klerry shouted, 'I loved playing chair bingo!' Lydia had won!

Lydia said, 'My favourite part was chasing Captain Blood with the other children and throwing him in the pool.'

Who or what Captain Blood was, I had no idea, but the girls couldn't stop laughing at the memory of the poor man toppling into the water.

It was heart-warming to see Mum and Dad through the children's eyes. I learned that the Donkey Derby was Granddad's favourite, and he volunteered to be a judge on the panel for the Lovely Legs competition. The girls' sense of humour was much like Dad's, so I imagined them all in stitches.

Lydia told me how on the car journey there and back they would sing 'Roll Me Over'. Luckily they didn't grasp the meaning of the racy lyrics because they were too busy looking out for their favourite building – it was shaped like a mushroom – and scoffing milk chocolate, which must have been Dad's doing, with that sweet tooth of his. How lucky I was to have such great parents, who were willing and able to help our girls create such wonderful memories when I couldn't.

Back to Win

Some years later, my friend Win and her husband Jim had to move to Blackburn, in Lancashire, for his work. Win was reluctant to go as it was so far away and we wouldn't be able to see one another as regularly as usual for afternoon teas, Sunday chats and so forth.

I was just as upset as she was but, of course, she had to go, and we promised we'd keep in frequent touch.

Win was quiet so it came as a pleasant surprise when, a week later, an envelope the weight of a small child came through the letterbox. It was from Win, who had filled seventy sides of A5 paper in her tiny neat handwriting. She sent letters like that two or three times a week and I would duly reply.

Other friends, especially those who weren't natural letter-writers, would ask in amazement, 'What on earth does she find to write about?'

As my writing style was the same, it was an easy question to answer. 'It's quite simple,' I'd explain. 'We don't need actual news to write a letter. We just write as if we were sitting together, having a natter over a cup of coffee.' Our letters back and forth were filled with comments about the weather, what we'd been up to, any plans we had. In time, we were referring to our letters as 'natters' because they were the next best thing to having one face to face.

Even our postman was bemused by the frequency with which Win wrote to me, and even more so when I told him the number of pages she would fill each time. 'In all the years I've been delivering mail, I've never had occasion to deliver as much from one person to another as I have from Win to you!'

Perhaps we should have asked if Win's natters qualified for a mention in *The Guinness Book of Records* . . .

A few years later, it was in a phone call that Win delivered some terrible news.

Jim had passed away. I offered my condolences, with heartfelt love and support. Win returned to letter-writing between sorting out the matters you have to deal with when a spouse passes away.

Eventually, I realized that Win was terribly lonely. At the time her son, Tony, was an articled clerk, studying to become a lawyer. He was living in London and would visit Win when he could, but as much as he wanted to help his mother move back to the south, he would be unable to do so for another couple of years. Win wanted to come back to live near us but it was financially impossible for her to make the move.

Unbeknown to Win, Stephen and I discussed asking her to live with us. We had to abandon the idea: if she moved in, and one of our parents, Aunty Ann or Uncle Ted, who were getting on in years – I was thirty-nine – needed to live with us, we couldn't face telling Win that she had to leave so that we could accommodate them.

We concluded that the best we could do was to tell Win she would be more than welcome to stay with us whenever she wished.

When I said so to Win, she accepted the invitation straight away, and for a few years, we spent quality time together twice a year. And she had two little girls whose company she could enjoy, Lydia and Klerry. She loved them as if they were her own granddaughters.

In March 1983, I went to the station to pick Win up. I waited excitedly on the platform, but when she came towards me, I was shocked at what I was seeing.

For all the years I'd known her, she had been trying to lose weight without success. I had done my best to reassure her that she wasn't overweight, just cuddly. She had a lovely face, with naturally wavy golden hair that she styled herself, and always dressed nicely. Now she had lost a lot of weight, but instead of looking slim and healthy, she looked ill. She gave me her usual lovely smile and hugged me tightly, but the sparkle had left her. She reminded me of a sad-eyed puppy. I hoped she wasn't ill, and that she hadn't detected any tell-tale sign on my face of the concern I felt for her.

Over the next few days, while Win was at our home, our face-to-face natters became heart-to-heart ones. She admitted she wasn't feeling well and that the weight had been falling off her.

'Have you been to your doctor, Win?' I pressed gently.

'Yes,' she said, 'but he was very dismissive and concluded I'm suffering with depression.' She told me, just as she had the doctor, that the only depression she was suffering was worry about her health. The doctor had refused to send her for more investigations. 'What if something serious is going on?'

While I didn't pretend to be a doctor, I'd spent years as a medical secretary. I had picked up the signs and symptoms in a patient that indicated the need for further investigation or referral to a consultant and I was sure Win needed medical attention. I vented my concerns about her to Dr Smallwood, who confirmed that I was right to be worried. He had always believed that it was most important for a GP to pay very close attention to everything a patient was saying, especially when that patient had been on a doctor's list for a long while without seeking repetitive consultations.

'So what can I do?' I said.

Dr Smallwood suggested I should write to Win's GP, telling him that, in the many years I had known her well, I had never known her to suffer from depression and that she was not one to bother the doctor with minor ailments. Most importantly, I should mention my anxiety about her current state of health.

When it was time for Win to return to Blackburn, she seemed even more upset than usual to be leaving us, and gave me an extra-long hug goodbye at the station. I so wanted to put her in the car and take her home with me and said as much. Win managed a little smile.

'I'd love that,' she said, 'but I have various things to sort out at home.'

I hugged her once more. 'Well, Win, as soon as you've done that, come back and stay as long as you wish.'

Win's eyes filled with tears and it was all I could do to hold mine back, at least until I had waved her off on the train. Then they began to flow. Poor Win. I allowed enough time for her to reach Blackburn, then telephoned to make sure she had arrived safely. She had and we signed off, Win promising to see the doctor again.

Days later, an envelope landed on our front doormat. I picked it up, saw Win's familiar handwriting, opened it and started to read. In the lounge, I flopped into the nearest armchair and my heart sank. In this natter, I could visualize the anxiety on Win's face, just as if she were sitting in front of me in the flesh. She wrote that, while she knew I had written to her GP with the best of intentions, he was far from happy about it and had made his feelings quite clear to Win: 'As and when I feel you need blood tests and/or investigations, I will institute them. I do not feel any are necessary, as I do not think that you are physically ill. I think you are suffering with depression.' She had reiterated that while she was feeling miserable it was because she was physically ill and wanted to know why.

Her GP had scribbled a prescription, pushed it across his desk towards her, and uttered two words: 'Take these.'

The pills turned out to be anti-depressants and sleeping tablets, medication she had never taken before and did not want now. Quite simply, Win rightly wanted an accurate diagnosis and the relevant treatment for whatever the problem turned out to be. The only thing her GP had succeeded in doing was to make poor Win feel even worse. Win asked me never to write to him again.

I telephoned her straight away to say how sorry I was that my well-meant letter had had the wrong effect, but added that she mustn't leave it at that. If she was reluctant to consult him again, she should ask for a second opinion at the surgery and, as far as I was aware, she could, by law, insist on a referral to the hospital. 'After all,' I told her, 'this is your life we're talking about.'

She was quiet and, shortly after, we said our goodbyes.

As usual, I wrote Win a natter in reply and posted it first class, as always. I had often wished that we didn't live so far apart but now I wished it all the more.

Because Win had written me such lengthy natters every few days for some years, I had expected her to put pen to paper as soon as she received my latest letter, as she usually did. I rather hoped it would prove therapeutic for her to get her thoughts and feelings down on paper to me. After all, a trouble shared is a trouble halved.

Two days passed and her letter did not appear on my doormat. The concern that had been gnawing away at me was now deepening. I tried calling and hoped her lack of an answer was because she had set off to the surgery for a second opinion or was out with friends in the hope it would cheer her up. I thought of her so many times during the day, and in bed at night, I would pray that she was being helped to get better, and that I would have a heartening natter from her soon to that effect.

Days later, Tony called. 'I'm sorry to tell you this, Linda, but Mum has been found dead in her bed.'

There was a scream and I realized it was mine. *Curse her GP,* I thought. He'd been so unkind and uncaring when all the while poor Win had been seriously ill, as I'd believed. I was distraught. Win's GP should be hauled before the GMC for gross negligence, I thought, and struck off.

But, as much as I loved Win, it was not my place to go down that route and poor Tony had more than enough to contend with. 'Please let me know if there's anything I can do to help, Tony. I'm so sorry for your loss.' But, like Win, I knew Tony would simply get on with things.

I went outside and stood by the globe light in the middle of the garden. The sun was setting and the soft light from the lamp gave the illusion of a full moon floating before me. Whenever Win had stayed with us she had stood in that spot and looked at the light. She'd loved it.

Next day, I went to the garden centre and bought a trailing yellow rose, Win's favourite flower. I planted it at the base of the garden light so that it would grow up and around the pole. Little did I know it, but yellow roses would come to have a significant meaning for me in years to come.

Already I was missing Win's and my natters. When the postman saw me a week later, he said, 'I haven't delivered one of Win's letters to you lately, Linda. Is everything all right with her?'

My eyes stung and I took a deep breath to calm myself. He put down his bag and stepped towards me. 'Oh, God,' he said, as I told him the sad news. He was close to tears himself as he offered his condolences.

Yellow Roses

The fifteenth of June 1983 started like any other normal day. I was meeting a friend and we were going out together. It had been nearly three weeks since Win had left us, and my friend had recently lost a loved one too. When she asked me to go to a special appointment with her, of course I agreed.

We went to the home of a woman called Mrs Young in Kingston-upon-Thames.

On our arrival, my friend introduced me and said, 'Would you mind if Linda waits here for me?'

'By all means,' replied Mrs Young.

It was a small house, and as she invited us in, she asked me if I would mind sitting on the staircase in the hall while she gave my friend her reading in the front room.

I took my seat and grabbed a magazine from the pile on the step below. I had read it from cover to cover by the time they emerged from the front room, my friend bleary-eyed. Mrs Young asked if I, too, would like a reading.

I had always been interested to know if there was anything to substantiate the idea of an afterlife, but I had never sought it. Now, as I stood in Mrs Young's hallway, I saw no reason to decline her offer. I smiled at her. 'Yes, please. I'd like that very much.' I went into the lounge and sat in the armchair she indicated. She reached for my hand and asked if she could hold one of my rings.

I had never taken my wedding ring off and didn't intend to. Instead I handed her a lovely ring that had been a Christmas gift from Stephen five years earlier – I wore it all the time.

'Please don't say a single word during my reading,' she said. 'You may have heard of mediums who say such things as "Someone is coming through whose name begins with the initial J," or "There is an elderly man who is not at all well." It is my belief that at that point the person having the reading starts racking their brain and offering suggestions to make the vague description fit. In either case, the medium is able to elicit information in such a way as to work around it. Sometimes they give the person hope that there is life hereafter.'

I stared at her, intrigued.

'By not speaking to me at all, you will know with absolute certainty that everything I relate to you is genuinely from those in the afterlife.'

I nodded.

She took a seat opposite me and moved my ring slowly between her right thumb and fingers. After two minutes, she looked intently to my right side. 'You have recently lost someone who was very close to you. She was not your mother but she loved you as if you were her daughter.'

The hairs on my arms stood on end but I did not make any indication to Mrs Young that she was right.

She described the woman, who fitted Win's description to a T, then said, 'She's standing next to you and will always walk beside you.'

Mrs Young's gaze moved across my lap. 'She's handing you a bouquet of yellow roses.'

My heart was racing. I looked to my lap, then to my side, hoping to catch a glimpse of what Mrs Young was seeing. I didn't, but tears were welling in my eyes. The oh-so-special someone I had recently lost was indeed my beloved friend Win, and yellow roses were her favourite flower – that was why we had planted the yellow climbing rose in her memory around the light she loved in our garden. As the tears spilled over, Mrs Young described the events that had led to Win's death. She paused, then shook her head. 'I'm sorry, she's gone away now.'

She went on to explain correctly that I had two daughters, each with an unusual name, who were both artistic. Lydia certainly was, but Klerry was still too young for us to really tell. Mrs Young told me one of the girls would go into the arts while the other would embark on a career in care. I remembered Klerry liked to play nurses. It was just as well Mrs Young had told me not to speak because I couldn't have even if I'd wanted to. I was absolutely speechless.

Then she said something that made me pipe up: 'You will come to be in a hot country, in a white house with arches, some place where oranges grow. After that, you will get better. I also see you surrounded by animals.'

I didn't know what she meant. 'I don't see how that's possible.'

I returned home deep in thought. I watched the girls closely and found myself imagining them many years down the line. Would Lydia become an artist? Would Klerry wear a real nurse's uniform and tend a ward of patients? Who knew? But one thing was for certain: I couldn't wait to find out.

Special Birthdays for a Very Special Man

After a childhood of quiet birthdays, I could now treat each one as truly special. Oddly, mine were of no consequence. All I wanted was the people I loved to enjoy their days. Because Dad so enjoyed company, especially that of his closest relatives and friends, his birthdays always felt that bit more special. We'd either go out for dinner or have a gathering at my home when, rather than sit down, Dad would stroll around making sure everybody had a drink and was happy. I would find myself watching him. How could anybody be sad when they had the pleasure of knowing Dad?

It was on one such birthday, his seventieth, that I realized just how important it was to acknowledge and celebrate the life of a loved one, not only on that occasion but every single day. That evening I was clearing up when the phone rang. It was Mum, her voice fraught with a tension I'd never heard in it before. 'Your dad's not breathing properly.'

I told her I was on my way and slammed down the phone, only to pick it up again and dial 999.

Minutes later, I arrived at Mum and Dad's house and flew faster up those stairs than I had ever moved in my life, taking them two at a time. I tried to rouse Dad, but no sooner had I started than two paramedics arrived in the bedroom. I realized I must have left the front door wide open when I'd rushed in.

I moved out of the way and one of them knelt down next to Dad, whose eyes were now open. 'Hello, pal. How are you doing?'

Dad smiled at the friendly stranger. 'Thank you.'

The ambulance man asked him a few more questions to assess his condition – about the weather, what day it was, what time of year. To each one, Dad had only one answer: 'Thank you.' Without further ado, he was taken to Kingston Hospital.

It was decided it would be best if Stephen, Mum, Lydia and Klerry stayed at home, while I went in the ambulance with Dad. I held his hand as the sirens blared and we raced through the traffic to the hospital. Every time Dad looked at me, he said, 'Thank you.'

No sooner had he been admitted to the hospital with a suspected stroke, than he clutched his chest and the alarms on the heart monitor beside him went berserk.

The resuscitation team crashed into the room. I leaped out of their way and went into a small waiting room nearby.

I was the only person in there and paced up and down, rather like I imagined expectant fathers did while they were anxiously awaiting the birth of their baby. I was praying for the safekeeping and continuation of a very special life. After what seemed an age, a doctor came into the room and I went to him, unable to resist the urge to hold on to his arm. 'My father?' I said.

He nodded. 'He had a heart attack but we resuscitated him and he's stable now. He'll need to stay in for a while so we can keep an eye on him.' He left the room quietly, and I looked up to the ceiling.

Now I was whispering, 'Thank you,' repeatedly. Many heartfelt thanks to the Big Man above, who had saved Dad's life.

I took my place at Dad's side. The stroke had been mild and he was now able to think straight and talk properly. I helped the nurse settle him comfortably and took over duties like giving him water so she could look after her other patients. Thankfully he made steady progress.

I stayed by his side until he was safely sound asleep, then drove home, so happy and relieved to be able to reassure Mum, Stephen and our daughters that Dad's outlook was good.

Just as I was about to climb the staircase to go to bed, I was stopped in my tracks by the sound of the telephone ringing. As it was so late in the evening, when usually only calls of an urgent nature are made, panic set in. Had there been a sudden deterioration in my dad's condition?

I grabbed the telephone receiver but, for a moment or two, hesitated to lift it to my ear for fear of what the caller was about to tell me.

When I braved it, the voice did not belong to an English nurse but a Chinese man. I immediately recognized it as belonging to Ma-Ong. He apologized for calling so late, but he felt sure that I would be eager to know that his wife, May-Ling, had just given birth to a beautiful baby daughter. 'Because your Klerry has been such a lovely friend to Siu-Fong and Chung-Man, we want to say thank you by naming our baby daughter after her. Are you pleased?'

Was I pleased? I was thrilled to bits!

I enlightened Ma-Ong about it being my dad's birthday and how scared we had all been at the thought of losing him. But that, thankfully, he was on the mend and would no doubt be thrilled to hear of baby Wong's safe arrival, especially on his birthday.

The fact that she was to be named in honour of his granddaughter would be the very tonic he needed for a complete recovery.

The following day, I rushed back to Dad's bedside and told him the news. He was over the moon and couldn't stop smiling.

Over the next few years May-Ling had another two daughters, naming one Linda, and the other Lydia. All three of us felt honoured, but nobody more so than me when May-Ling and Ma-Ong asked me to be godmother to all their five children. Of course, I was more than happy to accept.

First Sign of Trouble

At Christmas in 1983, we gathered at a relative's for lunch. Mum was sitting opposite me and, as we tucked in, something caught my eye. She was scooping her food from her plate, but instead of putting it into her mouth, she was tipping it on to her right shoulder. I caught her eye and mouthed: 'Are you OK?' I knew better than to ask out loud in front of everyone: Mum was stubborn as she was proud.

She nodded and mouthed back, 'Just tired.' She continued missing her mouth and tipping her food over her shoulder.

I got up from the table, draped my napkin over my chair and headed for the stairs.

Mum spoke up in her loudest voice: 'Where are you going, Linda?'

'I'm calling a doctor.'

'Don't you dare disturb him today of all days.'

I was soon dialling the on-call doctor's number.

He asked some questions, which I answered.

From what I had told him, the doctor was certain something had gone wrong.

I put the phone down and returned downstairs. Usually Mum would have been on her feet, pulling me to the next room and giving me a telling-off for calling the doctor. But she was confused and slow. I'd never seen her like that. When I helped her up and pulled her coat around her, she did grumble that she didn't like being jostled.

As Mum continued to protest, I got her into the car, clicked her seatbelt on and, with Dad and Stephen in the back, drove to the hospital. There, the Accident and Emergency doctor examined her, listened to the incoherent talk she was coming out with and she was admitted to the ward.

I stood in the middle of the room, the shock setting in. Dad wrapped his arm around my shoulders. 'She'll be fine, my lovely Linda.'

Dad's confidence should have reassured me. Only he didn't sound confident. He sounded scared. I turned my head to look at him, just in time to catch him wiping away a tear. I took his hand and led him to a seat. It wasn't the time for me to go into meltdown. Dad needed me. I sat holding his hand, and Stephen sat with his arm around my shoulders. Stephen was comforting me while I comforted Dad. In the midst of worry and despair, it was good to know that so much love surrounded Mum.

Some hours later, the doctor returned. 'Bett has had a stroke and a heart attack. She'll need to stay for a few days and be monitored.'

Beside me, Dad was shaking. The doctor left the room and quietly shut the door.

Dad was whispering something. I leaned in closer and heard him say, 'She's got to be OK. She's got to be

OK.' I hugged him close to me and Stephen held us both tightly.

Mum was very tired, so we sat quietly by her bedside until she drifted off to sleep. She used to say, 'Sleep is a tonic in itself,' so I hoped that she'd have a good dose of it and make a swift recovery. She did.

Summer came and Mum's health scare was a fading memory. Every Sunday, she and Dad came to us for lunch. Mum enjoyed sitting in the shade in the garden (the one thing she and I had in common was that we couldn't take the heat), while Dad revelled in the sunshine. Mum would leaf through popular women's magazines, while Dad read the Sunday papers.

On 1 September, Mum had been invited to the same relatives' house where she had been taken ill the previous Christmas. Although they had been visiting her over the months since that harrowing episode, they had been wary that the same thing might recur in their home and therefore they had, quite understandably, waited a length of time until Mum was much better before inviting her again.

Knowing she was in safe hands, I took the opportunity to pop round to her and Dad's house to give it a belated spring clean. Even though I was now a grown adult and a capable housewife, Mum still wouldn't let me do anything in her home.

Just then, there was a knock at the door. It was the relative with whom Mum was spending the day. His shoulders were slumped and his face pale. One look at him told me something terrible had happened. 'It's your mum,' he said. 'She's had a heart attack and been taken to hospital.'

Without a word, I followed him to the car and we rushed to Kingston Hospital.

Someone had telephoned Dad at the shop and he had jumped into his car straight away, arriving at Mum's bedside soon after us.

When the cardiologist had examined Mum he told us she had suffered a major heart attack and needed to stay in hospital for the necessary tests to be carried out.

Two weeks later, she was transferred to the Middlesex Hospital in London for heart surgery. Though Mum was putting on a brave face and enjoying having a little moan, she'd rub her chest and take deep breaths when she thought nobody was looking. She had pain, as you would after a heart attack, but she was too obstinate to admit it. She was fighting so hard and I felt proud of her – in the way a mother feels proud of her child. Strange how I could feel that now about my fearless mum.

While I had been able to get to Kingston Hospital every day to be with Mum, her transfer to central London meant that I encountered a big problem. I couldn't travel so far because of my panic attacks, but I felt guilty that I wasn't with her. A friend came up with an ingenious solution. One day he appeared with a work van and opened the back door. Inside there was a Portaloo. 'Knowing that's in the back, can you handle the hour's journey to see your mum?'

Grateful for his thoughtfulness, I flung my arms around him and thanked him. 'I'll try my best!'

I was a bundle of nerves the entire journey. The loo was in the back, but there was no way I could find the courage to ask him to stop so I could use it. By the time we arrived, I was terribly ill. My stomach was in knots and I was on the cusp of a panic attack. That was the first and last journey I made to see Mum at the Middlesex. I simply didn't have the courage to do it again. It was beyond my capability to make that journey into town. Thank Heaven my mum knew that my panic attacks were a genuine problem and that, without them, I would have been at her side every day.

Dad went every day and he, too, was very understanding about my problem, as he had been since it had begun. Most evenings, he'd return from the hospital and come to us for dinner. I was glad to see him every night and know that he was coping.

Eventually, after two and a half months in hospital, Mum was able to come home. Every few months, she'd return to her consultant for a check-up. He was called Tom Treasure and lived up to his name. He'd taken such good care of Mum and given her the very best of his skills and knowledge. I was so grateful to him that I wanted to do something in return. When I learned that his wife had had a baby, I scoured the shops for a present.

I was passing a quaint china shop when I found the perfect item. In the window there was a delicate money box. It was in the shape of a child's cot, complete with a blue blanket. 'My Little Treasure' was painted on it at the foot. I bought it and gave it to Mum, who loved it as much as I did. She opened her purse, pulled out a note and shoved it in. 'I'll give it to him tomorrow when I see him.'

When she returned from her appointment, Mum's eyes lit up when she recounted his reaction. 'Linda, it was wonderful. He thought it was lovely and said to thank you ever so much. It was an excellent choice.'

I felt rather chuffed about that, but after everything Mr Treasure had done for my mum, it was nothing but a tiny token to mark our gratitude.

After that, every time Mum saw him, she'd give him some money for the treasure box, either by sheer force or misdirection. Mr Treasure laughed at her cunning: she made sure her cash hit the inside of the money box and didn't somehow wind up back in her purse.

Time with Mum

One afternoon in the run-up to Christmas 1988, Dad had taken the girls for a wintry walk across the common while Mum and I were chatting in the kitchen. I sipped my coffee and Mum cupped a mug of tea in both hands. As I talked about my plans for the next day and the week ahead, Mum was looking at me in the most peculiar way. Now, she had always believed that if you look someone in the eye when you're speaking to them and shake their hand firmly, it shows you have a good strong character. But the expression in her eyes that day was one I'd never seen before. Sad? Scared? I couldn't place it. I asked what was wrong.

Mum replied, 'If I should wake up dead in the morning, I want you to know I've always loved you, Linda.'

For a moment, my mouth hung open, my stomach twisted and my mind raced away from me, from Mum, that house, this life and into God's garden where, all those years earlier, we'd buried Granddad Adams. In my mind's eye I pictured Mum next to him and I choked back a sob. I couldn't bear to hear Mum talk about her mortality. I didn't let emotion betray me. Instead I let a soft smile play on my lips. 'Do you know what you just said, Mum?'

She thought for a moment. Then she smiled too. 'Oh, yes! I won't wake up if I die, will I?'

I put both my hands around hers. 'Mum, you'd better wake up tomorrow because I've already made the lunch!'

She chuckled. 'OK, dear.'

As she left the room to go to the loo, I let out a breath and slumped back in my chair. Mum hadn't been well for a long time. Had she sensed something? Whatever her reason for saying what she had, I felt at peace. All my life I had wondered if, deep down, Mum really loved me. Though she'd proclaimed she'd wanted a daughter to call Linda, after I'd arrived, instead of indulging me with love and cuddles, she had been somewhat distant and closed off. She had always been the teller-off while Dad had been the hugs- and love-giver. Now something came to mind that I'd never really thought about. Before I was born, Mum had lost three babies to stillbirth. Had she suffered so much with my brothers' and sister's deaths that, somewhere in her heart, a wall had gone up? A wall to protect the ache of a grieving mother who had lost three babies before they'd had a chance to breathe, cry or smile?

God forbid, if I had been in her shoes, I don't think I'd have found the strength to keep trying for a baby. The fear of losing another child, the grief multiplying in that unbearable way, would have crippled me. Maybe Mum felt the same. Maybe she hadn't shown me closeness because she'd always been afraid of losing me. Maybe she knew, as I did now about myself, that she wouldn't find it in her heart to come to terms with a fourth loss of that magnitude. It certainly explained why, whenever any physical harm came to me, Mum would nearly lose her mind in a blind rage to keep me safe.

I sat at the kitchen table for a few more minutes, mulling over my thoughts and theories, my heart wibbling and wobbling in the strangest way. For the first time, I realized that Mum did love me.

A shout came from the living room, snapping me out of my thoughts. 'Linda! Put the kettle on, will you, please? I fancy another cup of tea.'

'Yes, Mum,' I said, then filled the kettle and hit its button.

Days later, I sent Stephen into the loft while the girls and I stood in a human chain below. Out came the boxes, each with a bit of tinsel stuck to it to mark the special items they contained: our Christmas decorations.

With a real tree waiting downstairs – looking a bit naked – and the smell of pine wafting around the house, I couldn't wait to get started. When the final box was down and the ladder stowed away, we grabbed what we could and headed for the lounge. We dressed the tree while Mum and Dad, who had come to stay for a few days over Christmas, sat side by side on the sofa. Their experienced eyes watched me, their only child who was now forty-four and had two daughters of her own to giggle alongside their father, the man they had long considered their son.

We larked about the tree and, occasionally, Mum or Dad would chuckle. Two hours later, the tree was ready. We went to bed, tired but happy, on Christmas Eve.

On Christmas Day, Lydia and Klerry were up early, eager to unwrap all their gifts, but they managed to contain themselves until Nanny Elizabeth and Grand-dad William joined us.

Again, Mum and Dad sat side by side on the sofa, beaming with delight as their granddaughters put on their Father Christmas hats and handed them their gifts. I took a lovely photo of Mum and Dad, dreading that this could be Mum's last Christmas, but never dreaming that she would be taken from us in just twenty-four hours' time.

We enjoyed such a happy Christmas Day. I slept soundly that night until a shuffling noise woke me, and a voice whispered, 'Linda, I'm sorry to disturb you but is my nurse coming?'

I looked at the clock. It was one in the morning. Nurses had been coming to see Mum daily since her heart surgery, to administer insulin injections, and I was baffled as to why she was now confused. I was too tired to find out. 'The nurse is coming, Mum, but not till later today. Why don't we get you back to bed for now?' I got up and took Mum back to her room where Dad was still sound asleep.

Next morning I went to check on her and she was awake but still in bed. Usually, the moment Mum woke she'd be up. She glanced at me and looked as weak as a kitten. What she said next confirmed it. 'Linda, I don't feel at all well.'

It was an extraordinary admission from Mum so I didn't hesitate in calling the district nurse. 'Please come as quick as you can.'

She arrived promptly, listened to Mum's chest and checked her pulse. Everything was normal. By now, Dad was awake and sitting beside her on the bed. He was so worried it broke my heart to look at them. Next to him Mum, who always had her lipstick on and her hair done, looked awful. Anybody catching sight of her now would never know this was the once glamorous, headstrong lioness Bett Peck.

After the district nurse had left, I took Mum into the bathroom and gave her a thorough wash. The doctor had advised us not to lift her into the bath so first I made sure the bathroom was nice and warm, then placed a fluffy towel across the toilet so Mum could sit comfortably while I washed her. She was quiet and lifted her arms when I asked her to.

She didn't even make a fuss.

Afterwards, I rubbed cream into Mum's legs, and she didn't protest at the grease or make a fuss like she usually would. The poor old sausage, I thought.

We were getting ready to visit relatives for lunch. 'Perhaps you'll feel better when we're there,' I said. 'It's only ten minutes away.'

She nodded.

When we arrived, I settled Mum into a comfy chair as everyone chattered around us. I wanted to tuck a blanket around her legs but thought better of it. She would have hated that.

After a while, a relative wanted to show me her new flat, which she had recently moved into. As it was nearby, I agreed to go. It felt good to be outside, strolling along in the crisp clear air, and we were soon on the way back – but as we rounded the corner to the house where everyone was gathered, I saw an ambulance outside it. I broke into a run, raced past it and knocked frantically on the front door. Someone answered, 'You can't come in.' The door was slammed in my face.

I was shaking as a horrible realization swept over me. Something so terrible had happened that everyone was under strict instructions to keep me outside. I paced up and down the front garden. Agonizing minutes passed, then the door opened and two paramedics carried a stretcher to the ambulance. The figure on the stretcher was Mum.

I gasped.

Dad was with them. I could see he was trembling and all thumbs as he tried in vain to help the paramedics load Mum into the back. My hands went to my mouth and I squeezed my eyes tight shut. As the vehicle's door slammed, leaving Dad standing on the pavement, my eyes flew open and I rushed to the paramedic, who was on his way to the front. 'Please follow behind us,' he said.

I nodded. But a voice in my head whispered: *She's gone. She's gone.*

*

Three months earlier, in October, I'd taken Mum to see her consultant for a check-up. It had been four years since she had undergone her heart surgery and, as she had become too frail to make the arduous journey into London, her follow-ups had been referred to Kingston Hospital. Her consultant examined her and read her notes, then told her to wait outside. Then he said to me, 'She needs more surgery.'

Mum and I had talked at length a number of times in the preceding weeks about what should happen if she needed more heart surgery. She'd told me over and over that she didn't want it. 'No matter what it means, Linda, promise me you won't let anyone take a knife to me. I can't go through that again.'

I'd begged her to have whatever treatment she needed, but my efforts to talk her round had been pointless. Mum was adamant. 'Never again,' she said. 'I won't have any more surgery, Linda.'

Mum's message was loud and clear: she'd had enough.

'Besides,' she said, 'what do I need more surgery for? My child is grown and my family is happy and set. I've loved my life, but when it's your time to go, it's your time. Quite frankly, Linda, if that situation arises, I don't even want to know, so please don't tell me. Just let me live out the rest of my days in peace.'

As she'd said it, she'd straightened her back, looked me in the eye and patted my hand. She knew what she wanted and, frankly, who was I to deny it? In any case, there was no arguing with Bett Peck.

Now, when the cardiologist asked me how I thought

we should proceed, I explained what Mum had told me earlier. He placed a hand on my shoulder and nodded. 'Realistically, I don't think your mother's heart will hold out longer than three months and I feel that she wouldn't get through another operation. But if she doesn't want to know, and is sure she doesn't want surgery, then it's up to you whether you tell her.'

I went outside and took Mum to the car.

She didn't ask me what the doctor had wanted to tell me and I didn't offer any explanation. She must have sensed the news had been bad but she didn't probe and I didn't tell another soul what I'd heard. Neither Dad nor Stephen would have been able to cope with the knowledge – Stephen was very sensitive and hated hospitals. Also, he was very fond of Mum. So, instead of sharing Mum's devastating prognosis, I carried on as normal, as did everyone around me because, of course, they were none the wiser.

Dad did all the housework and took care of Mum, who was growing weaker. Dad's GP advised him to get out of the house every day, even for a five-minute walk around the block, to keep himself in good health. Well, if Dad did go out, he'd race to the local shops but anxiety about Mum would make him rush back home, when Mum would say, 'Don't worry, Bill, I'm all right.'

But not even Mum could deny that she had changed. Though her hair was still perfectly coiffed and she wore her trademark pink lipstick every day, there was a resigned melancholy about her. She lost weight and the fight went out of her. She confided to me, 'When people look at me, they don't believe I'm ill, but I feel as weak as a kitten.' She said it as though she should feel ashamed.

I'd say to her, 'Those who know you will understand, and those who don't, well, it doesn't matter what they think, does it?'

Now, as the ambulance doors slammed in my face, I felt a rising panic. Her consultant had been spot on. It was Boxing Day 1988, three months on from his prediction. I thought, *This is it*.

Dad, Stephen and I got into my car, Dad sitting beside me, shaking and silent. We arrived at the hospital in time to see them taking Mum's stretcher into Accident and Emergency. We were shown into a family room and waited. Every so often, Dad let out a quiet whimper and I squeezed his hand. Finally, a doctor came in. 'I'm sorry, but there was nothing more we could for her.'

Dad went from whimpers to sobs. He bent double as they racked his body.

'Can't you give him something?' I asked the doctor. 'If you don't, he's going to have another heart attack.'

The doctor nodded and went out.

Dad was repeating the same thing over and over: 'It can't be true. She was all right. She can't possibly be gone – there must be something they can do.'

I didn't know what to say. My heart was broken at losing Mum and now all over again for Dad. When Dad finally sat down and put his head into his hands, he whispered, 'I can't go home without your mum, Linda.'

At that moment, Stephen took me aside. 'Don't worry, dearest, your dad will always have a home with us,' he said.

I hugged him tightly.

As we left the hospital, the sun had set and it was getting dark. People were going about their business, laughing, talking and wandering along arm in arm. It felt surreal. So much had changed yet everything was very much the same. I couldn't believe we'd lost Mum like that and so quickly.

I dropped Dad and Stephen at our home and went to Mum and Dad's house.

I didn't look at the armchair in the dining room by the fireplace. It was Mum's favourite spot and now it was empty. I went upstairs and packed a suitcase of Dad's essentials. He came to our home that evening and it would be fourteen years before he left.

Next day Dad and I went to say goodbye to Mum at the Chapel of Rest in Kingston Hospital. Mum was in a white dress, with a veil over her face. She looked quite lovely, rather like a bride. Dad stood beside her for a few seconds, then turned to me with a mix of hope and desperation on his face. 'Oh dear, Linda,' he began. 'They've made a mistake. Your mum's not dead. She's just asleep. Look how beautiful she is.'

I didn't have the heart to tell him otherwise. What was the point? Anyone who felt Mum's cold skin and watched, as Dad did, for the rise and fall of her chest would know the truth. He pulled up a chair, took her hand, visibly jolting at its chill, and talked to her in hushed whispers.

I stepped out to give him some privacy.

Later Mum was moved to the undertaker's premises and we began the difficult process of planning her funeral. We set the date for 5 January 1989. As Mum had loved Christmas, we kept the tree in our home, a wreath on the front door and lights about the garden.

Aunty Ann was inconsolable and in total disbelief. Then I had an idea. Dad and I took her and Uncle Ted to the undertaker's. I was certain that if she saw how lovely and peaceful Mum looked, it might ease her pain. She was willing to try so, hand in hand, we walked into the room where Mum lay. But as we neared her, Aunty Ann pulled me to a stop. 'I can't do it.' I put my arm around her shoulders and led her out. With tears in her eyes, she said, 'I'm so sorry, I don't know what came over me, but I couldn't see her like that.'

'Come on, let's go home.'

Mum had told me many times that she was a free spirit and couldn't bear the thought of being buried six feet under. Days later she was cremated and her ashes were scattered on her father's grave.

The last thing I could do for Mum was to make sure she had the send-off she deserved. Afterwards, everyone came back to my house for the wake. We talked about the good old days and my beloved dad, always the first to be there for anyone at a time of need, was thankful that so many people were there to support him in his. As painful as it was for him that his beloved Bett was gone, the only way forward was to celebrate Mum's life. We all raised our cups of tea – I'd got out my finest china – and toasted Mum. She would have liked that.

Next day, I took the Christmas decorations down, and Stephen put them into the loft. That night, as I hesitated outside Dad's bedroom, I heard his voice creaking with emotion as he talked to his wife. It broke my heart. As I slipped into bed, the pain, grief and tiredness of the last few weeks caught up with me and tears streamed down my face. Stephen enveloped me in his arms, stroking away my tears, and eventually I drifted into sleep.

After Mum

Even though I had grown up, got married, and become a mother, I'd still never had long hair. Without thinking about it, though, I stopped having it cut after Mum had passed away.

It was the late eighties and shaggy styles were fashionable: layers were cut into the hair, gel applied and then, using your fingertips, you tousled your hair. Almost before I knew it, my Italian cut had gone and my hair shimmied and swayed around my shoulders. Whenever I caught a glimpse of my newly grown locks in the mirror, I was reminded of those times when, as a child, I'd look at other girls' long hair with envy. Why had I waited so long to grow mine? Had Mum's message – nay, order – that you should wear a style that suited your face been so ingrained that my subconscious hadn't let me explore the opportunity? Whatever the reason, my hair was now much longer and I thought it looked lovely.

I was at a relative's wedding when I had an unexpectedly rude awakening. Aunty Ann, who would never have hurt my feelings for the world, came up to me with her usual warm smile. She fingered my hair and gave a sigh. 'Linda dear, I know you've always wanted long hair but, if I may say so, your mum was right when she said stick to the style that suits you.'

Hiding the pain her comment had caused, I was ready to explain how long I had waited to break free of Mum's rule.

But Aunty Ann continued, 'You always looked lovely with the Italian style and this one does nothing for you. It's such a shame.'

It was only because I knew she had had my best interests at heart that I could take her opinion with a pinch of salt and not be offended. Later, though, when I saw the photographs of myself at the wedding, I laughed. I showed them to Stephen. 'I think Aunty Ann was right in what she said about my hair!'

It had been a rather windy day and my hair looked like I'd been in a hurricane!

Since it was also rather thick, it was actually a right old mess. I imagined poor Mum gazing down from Heaven with That Look on her face. Now, at last, I could understand the reason behind it.

From then on, I took care to blow-dry my hair for special occasions or, indeed, at any time when I might fall prey to a photographer. By good fortune, Lydia and Klerry had both inherited naturally thick, wavy hair from me and their dad and they loved having long hair. Lydia's was dark brown and flowed past her shoulders, while Klerry's, also brown, was flecked with natural red highlights and went past her waist.

Lydia was now twenty and Klerry fifteen, and the

days of sitting with each of them at my feet while I spent hours brushing, plaiting, unravelling and replaiting their hair were gone. In my childhood, I had longed to spend hours like that with my mum, so when I had my two girls, I always found time to enjoy the simple moments in life with them.

Aunty Ann and Uncle
Ted Move Away

With Mum gone to the Pearly Gates, Aunty Ann and Uncle Ted decided to move to Dorset, where they had enjoyed many holidays over the years. In my childhood they had taken me with them to Bournemouth, Christchurch, Boscombe and the surrounding areas. All were lovely but my favourite was Lulworth Cove. It was on one of those visits that Aunty Ann recounted a story that made me burst out laughing.

'I asked if you were my real mum?' I said, amused by the notion.

Aunty Ann explained why I'd asked her that question, as we'd sat under a tree in her garden many years ago, and the memory of my curious theory came flooding back.

When I was a little girl, I'd thought that in the five years Uncle Ted had been missing, presumed dead, during the war, Aunty Ann had fallen pregnant after an indiscretion. It had led her to hand over the baby – me – to Mum and Dad to raise as their own. Now she told me exactly how true she'd been to Ted during their five years apart. I listened, astounded.

Aunty Ann and Uncle Ted had met in their teens, and it was easy to believe that, for them, it had been love at first sight. Petite Aunty Ann had had naturally wavy, long brown hair that framed her lovely face and twinkling blue eyes. Uncle Ted was tall, dark and devilishly handsome. Indeed, with a devilishly handsome husband of my own, I understood why Mum used to say, 'Looks aren't important but, gosh, don't they help?'

As well their good looks, Aunty Ann and Uncle Ted possessed thoughtful, kind, caring and loving natures. They always treated one another with love and respect that tended to rub off on those around them. I looked at them in awe from a young age, hoping I would be lucky enough to have such a happy marriage when I grew up. Eventually, of course, I was lucky enough to find my dear Stephen.

I shook off my thoughts as Aunty Ann continued telling her story.

They were twenty-one and had been married for only three months when the Second World War broke out and Uncle Ted was called up to fight for his country. Before long, Aunty Ann had received the dreaded telegram from the War Office, informing her that her beloved husband was missing, presumed dead. For the following five years, she continued to live in hope and prayed that one day Uncle Ted would somehow return safely to her. Meanwhile, she left her marital home and moved in across the road with my mum and dad.

In a similar situation, many young women accepted invitations to go out with men still at home or soldiers on leave, either for a night of dancing or a trip to the cinema. Later, of course, thousands of American GIs were stationed in England. The Americans were attractive in more ways than one. Not only were they handsome and romantic, they had an added advantage over the local men: they were comparatively well-off and could bestow gifts on women, such as stockings and chocolates, treats that were then beyond the means of the ordinary Englishman. There was one young woman, though, whom no one could persuade to 'fall by the wayside'. She received many invitations from young men who wanted to take her out but she politely declined them all. She preferred to stay at home, with a good book – Aunty Ann was an avid reader, with a special interest in history. She bided her time, continuing to hope that the day would come when she and Ted could build a life together.

Then came the day when there was a knock at the door. When Aunty Ann opened it, she stood rooted to the spot. There, standing right in front of her, was a weary-looking soldier. But all she could see was the same tall, dark, handsome young man with whom she had fallen in love and for whom that love had never waned, not even for a second.

Uncle Ted stood staring at his beloved wife, mesmerized by the vision of loveliness that met his gaze. Then my mum appeared on the landing and saw her sister and brother-in-law like two statues and called down to them, 'Don't just stand there! Kiss him!'

Now Aunty Ann was laughing and so was I.

That would have been a first for Mum, who was

extremely private when it came to matters of the heart and for whom a goodnight kiss on the doorstep was a definite no for fear of what the neighbours might say.

Aunty Ann and Uncle Ted fell into each other's outstretched arms.

When they had regained their composure, Uncle Ted stepped across the threshold and closed the door. While he and Aunty Ann held each other, Mum went into the kitchen to put the kettle on for a welcome cuppa. None of them was a drinker, but they all loved a good cup of tea, especially Uncle Ted who, in later years, was referred to affectionately as Tetley Ted by the youngsters in the family. No home was complete without a whistling kettle on the stove, he would say, always ready to make umpteen cups of 'cha'. Over the next few days he had talked about the traumatic events of the last five years, which to him had seemed never-ending.

But, Aunty Ann told me, he had believed his beloved Ann would be waiting for him, no matter how long the war took. It had kept him sane and intent on surviving so that one day he would go home to her.

It transpired that Uncle Ted had been captured by the Germans and taken to a prisoner-of-war camp in Italy. He had managed to escape, but with no more than the clothes on his back. At one point, starving, he had swapped his leather army boots for a crust of stale bread. Thankfully, many warm-hearted Italian people took pity on him, risking their own lives by welcoming him into their homes, putting him up and feeding him. One day, German soldiers hammered on the door of a house where he was taking refuge. The Italian family's plan of action was hastily put into effect.

Uncle Ted, with his back to the living-room door, hurriedly sat down in an old rocking-chair by the roaring log fire, with a large shawl to cover his head, shoulders, upper back and chest, and a blanket over his lap, legs and feet. He hunched his shoulders and rocked slowly, backwards and forwards, hoping against hope that the Germans would glance in his direction and mistake him for the family's grandmother.

The soldiers burst in through the front door. One rushed upstairs to check the bedrooms for any escapees hiding there while the other dashed in and out of the kitchen, front room and living room. They left as suddenly as they had appeared. The ploy had worked! Uncle Ted and his Italian saviours breathed a huge sigh of relief and gave thanks to God for having been on their side.

Aunty Ann explained it had taken Uncle Ted eighteen exhausting months to trek across Italy on his journey to freedom. But no matter how arduous his path was, he focused on the light at the end of the tunnel that would shine ever brighter in his wife's sparkling blue eyes and lovely smile.

As the news of his safe return home spread through the local community, people came to congratulate him on his bravery. After he'd had time to settle back into the family and had had plenty of much-needed rest, a welcome-home street party was held in his honour.

The local newspaper did a front-page article detailing the trials the war had inflicted upon Uncle Ted, and his resolve to come home to Ann, whatever obstacles were strewn in his way. It also told of her steadfast loyalty to her husband throughout the years when he was missing, presumed dead, and of her strongly held faith that God would answer her prayers to bring him home to her. A photograph of them, gazing into each other's eyes and smiling, warmed the hearts of even those who didn't know them.

'How marvellous it would be if your story was made into a film,' I said.

She laughed and shook her head, waving away the notion.

'Honestly, Aunty Ann, it's so inspiring. The cinemas would be packed, night after night, with people who, like you and Uncle Ted, were separated for so long.'

She couldn't see it, but I could.

One thing was for sure. The time they had spent apart, while the country was at war, had served only to strengthen Aunty Ann and Uncle Ted's love. It had paved the way for them to live the rest of their lives in the joy of their never-to-be-forgotten reunion.

I always returned home buoyed by spending time with Aunty Ann and Uncle Ted, but it wasn't long before that changed. Uncle Ted was diagnosed with stomach cancer, a rare form that was inoperable and wouldn't respond to any treatment. His prognosis was two to three months. The whole family was devastated; all any of us could do was to provide him and Aunty Ann with loving support.

During the weekdays, retired members of the family and those who didn't work took it in turns to be with Aunty Ann and Uncle Ted, staying with them for a few days at a time. I could drive to them at the weekends in a van Stephen had thoughtfully bought me, with the infamous Portaloo in the back. I enjoyed driving and felt relaxed on my way to and from Dorset so I never needed to use it. More than anything I was glad to be there for the aunt and uncle who had always been there for me.

Three months passed and Uncle Ted was still with us but, sadly, things went from bad to worse. He went on to develop Parkinson's disease, Alzheimer's, kidney failure and had a series of strokes, rendering him unable to walk or speak.

On one visit, after he hadn't spoken for months, we were watching an old film he used to enjoy: *King Kong*. At one point Uncle Ted turned to me and said, 'Kong.'

'Are you trying to say *King Kong*?' I asked. I didn't get an answer but I shot out to the shops and got the video for him. He could enjoy it every day if he liked. I also bought him a collection of black King Kong cuddly toys and placed them around his room. 'Kong' was the last word he ever said.

Eventually Aunty Ann moved back near to us all and placed Uncle Ted in a nursing home nearby so that the family could take care of them both. She wasn't allowed to stay with him overnight but was at his side from dawn until dusk every day.

One night, the call came. Uncle Ted had slipped away. To the amazement of the doctors, Uncle Ted had survived not just two to three months but more than two years. All of those who loved him saw his passing away as the end of his intolerable suffering.

I broke the news to Aunty Ann and wished I could erase her pain, take it all away. Relatives drove us to the home so that she could say goodbye to him. In the car, after a long silence, she asked, 'Linda, what did Uncle Ted really die of?'

We hadn't told her he had stomach cancer. If she had known, she would have dropped dead of fright. His consultant and their GP advised us to tell her from the outset that Ted had a stomach ulcer.

Now I couldn't answer her. 'Don't worry, dear,' she said. 'I think I already know.'

Over the following nine years, all the family did their utmost to try to fill the aching void in her broken heart. Tragically, Aunty Ann herself fell ill and was diagnosed with an aortic aneurysm and cancer. She put on a brave face and never complained, so when she telephoned to tell me that she was in a lot of pain, I jumped into my car and was with her in less than ten minutes.

She was admitted to St George's Hospital in Tooting. The consultant examined her and, from outside the curtain around her bed, I heard him say she might rally. He'd no sooner spoken than Aunty Ann's breathing became shallow. Although her lovely smile had faded and the twinkle had gone from her blue eyes, her gaze remained fixed on mine. I slipped my hand under her cheek and stroked her arm with the other. 'Thank you, Aunty Ann, for always being so wonderful. You and Uncle Ted were like another mum and dad to me. I love you beyond words and always will. You can be with Uncle Ted again now.'

Her chest stopped moving and, just like that, she was gone.

For no reason I could fathom, an old saying popped into my head: *Don't cry because it's over, smile because it happened.*

Thoughts of the many lovely happenings that she and Uncle Ted had brought into my life ran through my mind and I smiled, despite the tears streaming down my face.

Time with Dad

Now my girls had gone into the big wide world and were leading their own lives, separate from Stephen and me. Dad must have sensed I was having a tough time. 'My lovely Linda,' he said, one Saturday morning, 'it's such a beautiful day. Let's you and me do the food shop, then go for lunch somewhere.'

We set off.

Stephen was working weekends so Dad and I took our time. We stopped at the garden centre after the supermarket for a cup of tea. As we chatted across the table, I realized something. All my life, Dad had worked Saturdays. Now I was finally getting to enjoy quality time with him. It was like I was getting to know him all over again. Thereafter, every Saturday, we set off for local car-boot sales where we'd slowly work our way around, laughingly wondering if we'd come across a valuable antique.

One fine day, *Antiques Roadshow* came to Hampton Court. We always enjoyed watching that on TV so I was thrilled that it was coming to a venue to which I could drive Dad. We were like excited schoolchildren when Michael Aspel and John Bly came up to us. 'What antique do you have for evaluation?' John asked.

I laughed. 'My dad!'

A bemused John Bly replied, 'I'm sure he's priceless!'
How right he was.

Sometimes Dad and I took little drives around Morden, and anywhere that we thought looked nice, we'd stop off for tea or a bite to eat. Often, Dad would pick a garden centre. There was one unspoken rule for our outings and that was that we would stick close to home. Dad was always mindful of my limitations. But as much as I enjoyed the quality time, and I'm sure Dad did too, the rawness in his grief over Mum was never far from the surface. We'd be chatting when something would happen and Dad would say, 'I must tell your mum about that.' He'd stop suddenly, as the realization that she was gone swept over him. Sometimes, he'd fall silent. At others he'd cry. It was heart-breaking.

I was working full time and so was Stephen. We put in long hours and returned in the evening to cook a meal and watch telly with Dad. Though Dad watched the football with Stephen and old films with me, it wasn't enough. I even talked to Stephen about getting a dog to keep Dad company, but decided that it wasn't fair to place such a responsibility squarely in Dad's lap. He wasn't so young and perhaps it would be too much.

It wasn't long before a novel solution presented itself.

Out of Retirement

Dad and I were out one day, having a cup of tea in a lovely quiet café we'd happened upon, when a man came up to us. He put a hand on Dad's shoulder. 'Bill?'

Dad's eyes lit up. 'Jimmy!' he said, rising to grasp the man in a big bear hug.

Dad knew Jimmy Powell from years earlier when Jimmy had owned a greengrocery in Wimbledon. However, reconstruction there had meant that he'd had to relinquish the shop and now he had a fruit and vegetable stall at the foot of Wimbledon Hill. He'd been renowned for having the best fruit and veg – even the official buyers for the Royal Household knew of him. Now, as the two men reminisced about the good old days, and tussling over the freshest fruit and veg at Covent Garden before most people had got out of bed, there was a spark in Dad that I hadn't seen for months. On learning of Mum's death, Jimmy's smile faded and he patted Dad's shoulder. 'I know how much you loved Bett,' he said.

Dad nodded, too choked up to speak.

Jimmy was quiet for a moment. Then his hand flew to his chin and he began to talk. As Dad listened, his whole face changed. He made a fist and lightly thumped the table. 'Jimmy, that's a wonderful idea,' he said. 'I'd love to help out on your stall.'

With Dad's recent health, I wasn't so sure it was a good idea but on Monday morning, he was up and dressed, shaved and ready to go at six thirty – a late start in his book. We set off in my car, and I dropped Dad at Jimmy's stall, then drove on to work. I worried about him all day. What if he couldn't take the long hours on his feet? What if his blood pressure went up? At six o'clock, I pulled up by Jimmy's stall and Dad strolled towards me. He had a spring in his step and the familiar sunny smile on his face. I beamed back at him. He opened the door and got in with more bounce than I'd seen in him for donkey's years. 'Well?' I said.

'Well what, my lovely Linda?' he said, with a grin. 'I'll tell you what. That was the best day I've had in a long time. Will you drop me off same time tomorrow?'

There was no point my telling him again that I was worried about his health. Instead, I said, 'Of course.'

Before long Dad was working six days a week. Everybody loved him, and although he was working for Jimmy, he had such a polite and friendly manner that many customers thought he was the stall's owner. Just as he had pulled Aunty Ann out of her depression years earlier, now Jimmy was doing the same for him.

When I pointed that out, Dad smiled. 'Funny how life goes full circle on you sometimes, isn't it?'

I never heard Dad complain, and I often bit my tongue to stop myself telling him off for working too hard or tiring himself out. Until one day he got into the car and let out a groan as he sat down.

'Are you all right, Dad?'

'I'm on top of the world, Linda.'

I gave him a sideways glance. 'No, you're not. What's happened?'

Dad chuckled at the inquisition but he relented, telling me he'd gone downstairs to the 'office' (which in days gone by had been a gentlemen's public convenience but was now completely refurbished) to make a cup of tea. As he'd taken the second to last step, he'd tripped and fallen, hurting his knee.

Now I was the one giving Dad one of Mum's looks.

He waved it away with his hand but I almost marched up to Jimmy to give him a good telling-off. I'd specifically told him that should Dad become unwell or have an accident Jimmy must call me from the payphone nearby, no matter how much Dad protested. Clearly, my instructions hadn't been followed and I knew why. Dad, the old charmer, could be most persuasive when he wanted to be. But so could I.

I took him to hospital and an X-ray revealed a hairline fracture in his right knee. The doctor bandaged it up and asked Dad if he had any pain.

'I'm on top of the world,' he said once more.

Next day, I picked Dad up from work – he'd insisted on going in. He was waiting in the usual spot, beaming from ear to ear.

Surprise!

While we marked all birthdays with a special meal out, milestone birthdays called for an extra special party. And Dad's eightieth birthday definitely qualified. As it loomed closer, I took a letter to Dad, in his favourite armchair by the fire, and placed it at his side.

He read the invitation to a silver wedding anniversary party for a couple we knew and his eyes shone. 'Oh, we'll have to get them something lovely,' he said.

Dad had taken the bait just as I'd intended. He didn't know that the invitation was a fake. There certainly was a party but it wasn't for a wedding anniversary. It was a surprise bash for Dad's eightieth that I'd been keeping under my hat.

Together, we went shopping for a gift and a nice card for the couple named in the invitation, who would indeed celebrate twenty-five years together – six months later than Dad thought! On the day, I wrapped the present and Dad signed the card, with seven kisses for luck, as always. Then we got into the car and, with Dad holding the gift in his lap, went to a nearby hall. He was dressed in his finest, and when we arrived, the couple who'd helped me trick Dad were waiting outside, as if to greet their guests. We embraced, sharing congratulations and kisses. But instead of sending us inside, they escorted us. As the double doors opened, dimmed lights were flicked on and a huge crowd of people rose to their feet to let off streamers and poppers. Dad stopped in his tracks as a familiar song blared out: 'Congratulations'!

He looked at me, clearly confused. Over the din, he shouted, 'For me?'

I nodded, and turned him round so he was facing the massive banner hanging above the door.

CONGRATULATIONS YOUNG BILL !

Everyone sang 'Happy Birthday', then 'For He's A Jolly Good Fellow', and gave three cheers for Dad.

Dad was glued to the spot, gazing around at all his family and friends in amazement.

They swarmed towards him, like bees to a honey pot, the men to shake his hand, the women to kiss him, the children joining in. To say he was chuffed was the understatement of the year.

Dad swanned around, talking to all the guests, some of whom he hadn't see in decades. He positively glowed with the thrill of seeing so many he'd not caught up with for so long. I followed him, snapping pictures of him with every group – mementoes I knew he would cherish after the event. Whenever I asked him if he was enjoying himself, he said, 'I'm on top of the world, my lovely Linda.'

As the evening went on, two birthday cakes were presented to Dad. One had 'Happy 80th Birthday Bill' on it in navy blue, and the other depicted a horse-race – because Dad loved a flutter. He was thrilled to bits and beamed as the 150 guests sang 'Happy Birthday' to him once more.

Afterwards, a microphone was handed to Dad and his favourite song came on.

As he began the familiar tune of Dean Martin's 'I'm Forever Blowing Bubbles', the children raced forward, armed with colourful bottles. They knelt at Dad's feet and blew bubbles at him. Dad stopped singing and started laughing. When he continued singing, surrounded by a cascade of bubbles, I took my camera and snapped one last picture. I felt fit to burst with happiness.

Finally, after a fabulous evening, I took Dad home and we nattered the whole way back. When we pulled up outside, I was about to open the door when Dad's hand grabbed mine. His eyes were shining. 'Thank you, Linda. That was the best party in the world and the biggest surprise of my life.'

I squeezed his hand. 'You thoroughly deserved it and it was my pleasure.'

A few days later, Dad was making a cup of tea for us before we set off to our respective jobs. Something pink caught my eye on the coffee-table. It was a bouquet of roses and, against the vase, a white envelope. On it, a familiar neat script read, *My lovely Linda and Stephen*. I opened it and read the card. Two lines were printed on the front, both of which Dad had underlined:

> *Because you've been so very kind, so very thoughtful too,*
> *This little note just comes to bring a grateful thanks to you.*

Inside, Dad had written:

To dear Linda and Stephen,

*Thanking you for the surprise of my life on my 80th Birthday.
The Party was No. 1 in the Charts.*

Our Love, as always, Dad xxxxxxx

My eyes pricked with tears. Even now, years after Mum had passed, Dad always wrote 'our' to include his Bett.

I placed the card beside the vase, went to Dad and hugged him. No words were needed or exchanged.

At the age of eighty-three, Dad was still working hard for Jimmy and was a favourite with all the customers. He'd joke with the ladies, 'If you can guess my age correctly, I'll pay for your fruit and veg.'

There was one particular customer he adored. Every week, a blind lady would come for her stash of fresh goodies but it was not she who delighted Dad: it was her Golden Retriever, a trained guide dog. When he wasn't working for his owner, he'd eye Dad for a sneaky treat. Dad would be ready and waiting with a handful of doggy delicacies he'd bought. You're not supposed to give treats to working dogs, but Dad, having checked with the owner, loved to watch him enjoying them. In whichever direction Dad threw the treats, the dog would snap them up, never once leaving his spot by his owner. Dad laughed every time and so did the other customers.

I reckoned it was my dad's playfulness and sense of fun that led to him winning an award from the Stroke Association, which was written up in the local paper. He was an inspiration to all around him and now he had a certificate to prove it once and for all. Of course, I'd nominated him. When Dad saw the piece in the paper, he held it under my nose and pointed at his age. 'I suppose this means I can't play the guess-my-age game any more, eh? I'd be paying for everyone's fruit and veg!'

His age wasn't the only thing Dad made light of. As he grew older and became hard of hearing, he had numerous hearing aids, ever hopeful of improving matters. Sometimes one helped but, inevitably, he'd have to return to his GP for it to be adjusted. The GP would return Dad's smile. 'Captain, you really should accept that your ears are eighty-five years old!'

Dad, still smiling, would cup one ear and turn that side of his head to the doctor. 'What was that you said, Doctor?'

We'd all burst out laughing.

The GP, who had been Dad's doctor for many years, would refer him to St Helier Hospital for another hearing test. There, Dad's shenanigans would continue. The technician would sit Dad in a soundproof glass booth, hand him a buzzer and say, loudly enough for Dad to hear, 'Mr Peck, I'm going to play some music for you. When you can hear it, I'd like you to press the buzzer, please.'

On one occasion, the moment she closed the door

and went to stand behind a screen, about to start the music, a red light atop the booth Dad was in would be flashing. I did my best to avoid the technician's eye: Dad was pressing the buzzer quite clearly before the music had begun. From the growing bemusement on the technician's face, I felt sure she'd realized what I already knew – Dad was cheating!

After the test, we looked at him in the booth and noticed that, although the music had stopped, his finger was still pressing the buzzer. When the technician opened the door, Dad asked, 'Did I pass the test with flying colours?'

She smiled broadly and replied slowly, clearly and loudly, 'MR PECK, YOU ARE DEAF!'

Dad was still smiling and, from the way the corners of his eyes were crinkling, I could tell he was suppressing the mother of all laughs. Dad might have lost his hearing, bless him, but he would never lose his lovely smile. I grinned because his smile was infectious.

Rock Bottom

No matter what was going on with Dad, whether it was a trip to the dentist or a more unpleasant examination, I insisted on taking him myself. He'd resist and implore me to let him get on with it. 'Really, my lovely Linda, you don't need to trouble.' Nevertheless I'd book time off work and accompany him.

Once, I was sitting in the hospital while Dad was examined in the consulting room across the corridor. Suddenly a startled '*Ooh!*' echoed in the waiting room. I thought, Oh, poor Dad. From the expressions of the patients around me, it was apparent their thoughts were running more to the tune of 'Poor me'!

As I watched, their anxious looks turned into bewilderment. Dad was singing one of his favourite songs: 'I'm Forever Blowing Bubbles'. The words floated through the air, like bubbles, and his voice ranged from strong tenor to soprano, which indicated dynamic changes rather well. No explanation was necessary.

Once Dad's rectal examination had been carried out, the consultant, Nick Bett, called me in with a playful grin. I'd worked many Saturday mornings for him at his home so I was familiar with his light-hearted nature. I'd got to know and like him, and his wife, Penny, very much.

Those mornings had been a pleasure as they owned two beautiful Labrador Retrievers, Sindy (an abbreviation of her kennel name, Midnight Cinderella), and Saffron, or Saffy, a yellow one. When I entered the house, they ran around my legs, welcoming me, and then, as Nick showed me to his office upstairs, Sindy and Saffron dashed up alongside us and promptly took up their positions, one sitting at either side of the office chair. For me, those Saturday mornings couldn't come quickly enough. I was like a child let loose in a toy shop. On the way to Nick and Penny's, I would stop to buy some treats for the dogs, as a thank-you for keeping me company while I typed merrily away. It was not as though they needed treats from me – they were given more than enough by their master and mistress, who loved them just as if they were their own grandchildren – but I couldn't resist spoiling them a bit more.

Now Nick said, 'I've heard many patients undergoing a rectal check mutter under their breath or let out an *ooh!* But, believe me, I've never heard one sing before!'

I could only imagine!

As we left the waiting room, Dad, as always, doffed his hat, tipped his walking stick slightly upwards and bade the other patients, 'All the best, be lucky!'

I'd done my best to research the doctors and consultants Dad would visit if ever the need arose, and when he heard which surgeon would fix the carpal tunnel syndrome in his hand, Dad was rather surprised. 'If he's good enough to operate on royalty, he's good enough to operate on you,' I said firmly. 'After all, you're always saying, "Nothing but the best is good enough for my lovely Linda," so nothing but the best is good enough for my lovely dad.' To which he gave me a tight hug.

While those Saturday mornings with the Betts are long since over, it's good to know that Nick and Penny have taken two new Labrador Retrievers into their home and hearts. The black one's kennel name is Galaxy Twirl and the yellow one is Cream Egg, but Nick and Penny call them Sparkle and Sunshine respectively. Little did they know that, several years ago, I'd bought a lovely black kitten, for good luck, as a new-home surprise for our friends Irene and Ralph – I'd known they wanted one – and they'd named her Sparkle, while one of our sandy-coloured cats is called Sunshine. Great minds think alike!

Mamma Rosa

After fourteen years with us, Dad moved to a retirement complex with round-the-clock wardens, nurses and carers on hand if he needed help. I had been worried about the move, but Dad loved his cosy new flat. He was still fiercely independent and rarely called for a carer to help him with anything. Instead, he revelled in having his own space again.

One day when I went to visit, Dad told me he'd met a lovely lady called Rosa. 'She wants to meet you, Linda. Will you come and see her with me today? I know you'll adore her.'

I nodded. Dad stood up and led me to a flat two doors up. We knocked and a voice called us in. Rosa was sitting by the window facing us, her white hair in soft curls and a smile so lovely it warmed my heart. She wore a long string of pearls, had had a French manicure and looked very glamorous indeed. She made me welcome and it was obvious from the first moment that she had a very sharp mind. We immediately took to one another, just as Dad had promised.

From that day on, every time I went to see Dad, I stopped in for an hour or two with Rosa. Only when Dad was hospitalized was it just Rosa and me. Gradually I learned about her past.

Rosa had been born in Hungary to Jewish parents in January 1920. When she was nineteen, they had sent her to England to avoid the increasing dangers posed to Jewish families by the Nazi regime. In London, she had met and married Johnny, the love of her life, and their daughter, Sonia, a honeymoon baby, was born within a year of their marriage.

After Sonia had arrived, Rosa had suffered seven miscarriages in seven years until, finally, she gave birth to her second daughter, Caroline. How happy they were.

All too soon, however, tragedy struck again. At the age of twenty-four and having been married for only three months, Caroline died from cancer. I thought of Mum, who had lost babies too. How terribly sad it was that so many women suffered in that way.

By now, Dad was ninety, but that didn't mean his cheeky ways had stopped.

One day, I went to see him and found his room empty. I had a pretty good idea where he'd be. Mamma Rosa, as I was now calling her, had recently moved to the flat opposite Dad's so I went across the hall and knocked on her door.

'Come in!'

I went inside and there, in the two armchairs overlooking the balcony and manicured gardens, were Mamma Rosa and Dad, chatting and giggling together. It was an endearing sight. 'Hello, you two,' I said.

'Hello, my lovely Linda. You know my girlfriend?'

Well, that had us all in stitches.

Mamma Rosa kept a dish of fruit drops for Dad on

her sideboard, which was otherwise filled with pictures of her family. Dad treated her to flowers to make the room 'smile'. They spent every day together for six years, watching TV, filling in quizzes side by side and reminiscing about the good old days. Sometimes they'd even have a sing-song. Mamma Rosa had gone straight into Dad's heart and, not so surprisingly, straight into mine.

Then something happened to pull the rug from under us. Dad fell and broke his hip quite badly. I arrived at the hospital as the surgeons were about to set to work fixing it.

The consultant came to me. 'Because of his heart, there is a significant risk of your father not making it through this operation.' I nodded and told him to do what he could to save Dad. The team set to work and I paced the corridors anxiously.

Finally, there was news. Good news. Dad was in the recovery suite. When he was back on the ward, it was past visiting hours but, frankly, I couldn't have cared less. I sat at his side as he slept.

In the ward, a doctor appeared to check Dad's condition. 'Your father survived the operation but his blood pressure has gone through the floor. Do you think you could stay with him tonight? It might help.'

Could I? 'You'll have trouble getting rid of me,' I joked weakly.

I sat beside him all night. I didn't sleep a wink and talked to Dad in quiet whispers until the sun came up. Dad was still out for the count, but when a nurse came to make some checks, she smiled. 'You must be some sort of medicine, Linda,' she said. 'Your father's blood pressure's looking a lot healthier today.'

Dad was ninety-six and still fighting.

When he came round, it was as if the sun was shining full force in my face. He beamed and so did I. I told him, 'I love you, Dad.'

'Me too, my lovely Linda.'

In time, Dad was able to return to his flat and did well to recover from his surgery.

But after a while I noticed that he was beginning to repeat things. Other times he'd get muddled and mix people up. He'd call Klerry Lydia, and vice versa. At first, I didn't think too much of it. After all, Dad was ninety-six. But when it became much worse, to the point that he sounded like a scratched record, repeating one line of a song over and over again, I took him to his GP, who referred him to a specialist.

During the appointment, I sat quietly while the consultant questioned Dad. I soon saw that he was going through a standard assessment for Alzheimer's. Afterwards, he gave his diagnosis and I felt the colour draining from my face. It was Alzheimer's and it was advancing.

Dad and I returned to his home, Dad confused and quiet. I was devastated.

At home, Stephen and I talked for a long time about how I would cope when I lost Dad, which, until now, I hadn't dared think about. But although Dad's body was still with us, his personality and memories were already slipping away. Stephen held me tightly as I cried.

What else could be done? Sadly, nothing.

Over the course of the next year Dad needed more help and support than his current home and wardens were able to give so he moved into a nursing-home with specialized carers. The goodbye between him and Mamma Rosa was short and sweet, neither of them able to fathom the distance that would soon lie between them. I visited both as often as I could, usually going to Mamma Rosa's when Dad was asleep. On Fridays and Saturdays I treated her to a pot of the jellied eels she loved, just as I did for my dad.

One day, I got a call that brought a smile to my lips, even if it did make me worry a bit. I went in to speak to the management at Dad's home. They told me, 'Your father keeps sneaking out to get the bus. One of our carers happened to bump into him in Elephant and Castle and brought him home.'

'Oh dear,' I said. 'Leave it to me.'

I went to Dad's room and he beamed at me. 'Dad, why do you keep getting on the bus?' I asked.

'I want to go home and see my mother, Linda.'

Of course his mum had died long ago. But after much toing and froing I realized that by 'home' he didn't mean my house or his old terrace with Mum: he meant the home where he'd been born, in Elephant and Castle.

Then I had an idea. I took Dad for a drive and started heading into town. On the way he admired the sights and, if we drew to a stop in traffic and a lady looked at him, he'd doff his hat, as always. We spent hours in the car that day, Dad admiring the view, me secretly searching for Thomas Doyle Street. After circling the area it should have been in for what seemed an eternity, I stopped and asked workmen for directions. One said the street no longer existed. He must have seen the disappointment flash across my face because he added, 'It's now called Earl Street.'

Well, I was off like a flash. I was so excited. I envisaged knocking on the old red door, number twenty-eight, Dad had described to me, but when I finally came to where it should have been, my heart sank. The terraced home that clearly meant so much to him was no longer there. In its place there was a row of newly built houses, plus a couple of towering office blocks.

I drove past without uttering a word and prayed Dad wouldn't recognize where we were.

He didn't. And who could blame him?

By now, Dad was getting anxious. He was tired. 'I just want a cup of tea.' I offered to stop at the next café we came across, but he said, 'Thank you, my lovely Linda. Let's go home to have it.'

I drove back to Mitcham and as we pulled into the gates of the nursing-home, Dad smiled. He said, 'We're home.' I hadn't told him where I'd been hoping to take him that day and now he didn't ask any questions. 'Thank you, my lovely Linda. That was a nice drive. I always enjoy seeing the London skyline.'

I took him back to his room and settled him in his armchair. Then, as he enjoyed his cuppa with his custard creams, I drank a welcome mug of coffee and put the TV on. *Deal Or No Deal* was beginning, and although Dad's mind was no longer as sharp as it used to be, I encouraged him to join in the quiz shows. We would each choose a box number and wait eagerly to see if we had picked a winner. I always stayed with him until he was tucked up in bed and had fallen asleep. Then, thinking back to those nights when I was a girl and our roles were reversed, I would kiss his forehead and whisper, 'Good night, God bless, my beloved dad. I love you beyond words and beyond eternity.'

As I made my way to the car, one of his carers called for me. She pulled me aside and began to chat. I waited patiently till she got to her point.

'It's lovely that you took your dad to Elephant and Castle today. Some weeks ago, I was there running errands when I saw him stepping off the bus, looking lost and confused.'

She was the person who'd found him. 'I tried to calm him down and eventually convinced him to get back on the next bus. We stood in the queue, and when it arrived, your dad let all the ladies on first. When they remarked on what a gentleman he was, he told them he had to be otherwise his dad would tell him off!'

I laughed. Typical!

'I just thought I'd tell you,' she went on, 'because so many relatives worry they're losing their mum or dad or whoever comes to us here at the home. But I promise you, somewhere in there, they're still there and it's those moments of clarity, or flashes of their old personality, that tell us.'

Her words brought tears to my eyes. It was a comfort to know that not all was lost.

A Century to Celebrate

In spite of all he had been through, Dad was in relatively good general health as his ninety-ninth birthday approached so I decided to give him an extra-special surprise party. I made a reservation at the Kiss Me, Hardy restaurant where we had enjoyed many lunches together. Like a child let loose in Aladdin's Cave, I had great fun wandering around a local party shop, choosing bits and bobs, including a birthday badge for Dad to wear on the smart new suit I'd bought for him. There was also a crown for him to wear, a nod to Dad's old joke that his mother had named him William James after many kings of England, as well as the usual party decorations to adorn the seating area that would be cordoned off for us.

The party-shop assistant went to the venue ahead of us on the day to put the decorations in place, including a large display of blue and yellow balloons (a nod to the dress my mum had worn on the day they first met), used to make '99', on either side of the entrance to where we would be seated. I arranged for a special ninety-ninth birthday cake: one '9' was a fruit cake and the other a sponge to cater for all tastes. Each was decorated with items that would mean something to Dad, from a black cat for good luck to fondant fruits that represented the years he'd spent as a greengrocer.

The evening went well, with Dad completely surprised. We were careful not to repeat what might have led to a dangerous situation when we'd celebrated Dad's ninetieth birthday. That time, the waitress had approached Dad, carrying his cake with all the candles flickering. Everyone stood up to sing 'Happy Birthday' and 'For He's A Jolly Good Fellow' and, as loud cries of *Hip, hip, hooray* rang through the air, they were suddenly drowned by a loud siren. For a split second, my first thought was of how quickly I could get Dad out of danger. Then we realized what had happened. The enormous number of burning candles had created enough heat to set off the smoke alarms! The candles were hastily blown out, by Dad and others, and there were sighs of relief all round.

Throughout his ninety-ninth birthday party, I was hoping and praying that my beloved dad would, as he so desperately wished, live to celebrate his hundredth birthday and receive his card from Her Majesty The Queen.

The Hundredth Birthday

As in previous years, I wanted to give my beloved Dad a party to celebrate his birthday, but, this being the hundredth, which he had in latter years often told me he felt sure he would live to see, I naturally wanted it to be the most special of them all, especially as, to me, he was the most loved centenarian of them all.

However, four months prior to that oh-so-special date, he was admitted to hospital, suffering from pneumonia. At the time of his admission, he walked into that hospital but, during the time he spent there (just under a month), he developed chest and urinary infections and lost so much weight that he was unable to walk again, and needed a permanent catheter, resulting in the recurrent urinary tract infection, which would, in due course, be certified as the primary cause of his death. His general practitioner was wonderful and attentive, doing the best he could for my dad, but he explained that, due to Dad's advanced age, it was now too late for any amount of physiotherapy to enable him to walk.

For a man who had been so amazingly stoical, always doing his utmost to be independent and not be a trouble to anyone, this was a nail in his coffin. Even then, though, his eyes would occasionally light up, he would smile his lovely smile, and utter the immortal words, 'You're my lovely daughter, my lovely Linda. I love you more than anything in this world, and I'm happy when you're with me.'

Because my poor dad's physical state was such, I didn't dare make firm arrangements for his hundredth birthday, worrying that I would be tempting Fate. However, with a few days to go, I contacted his nearest and dearest and explained that I would be laying on a buffet in the day room at Eltandia, the home where he lived, and that they would be more than welcome to come and celebrate this wonderful man's life with him. I ordered a bespoke hundredth birthday cake, depicting all aspects of things he enjoyed in his life, balloons and special banners with which to decorate the room. I also bought him a smart new suit, and a silk tie dotted with Swarowski crystals. It didn't matter that he would only ever get to wear it once. Throughout my whole life, my dad had wanted 'nothing but the best for my lovely Linda', and, where I was concerned, there would be 'nothing but the best for my beloved dad'.

I sat with Dad until past midnight on 19 January 2012 so that I would be there to wish him a happy birthday when he woke up. I kissed his brow, saying, 'Well done, my beloved dad! You've made it to see the hundredth! Heartiest congratulations and happy birthday! God bless you!'

I then drove home 'to hit the feather', as Dad would have said, and to give thanks to God for having granted him his wish to see his hundredth birthday, before catching a few hours' sleep so that I would awake refreshed to give him as happy a day as I possibly could.

Nothing could lessen the warmth I felt in my heart that day. As I entered Eltandia, I could not have wished for a more welcome sight. My dad, having been washed and dressed in his new clothes, was in his wheelchair, being pushed towards me, with the crown I had bought from the Party Shop sitting proudly on his head. Crown or no crown, he would always be a king to me. He was wheeled to the furthest half of the day room, sectioned off by the buffet tables, and his chair came to a stop in front of his hundredth birthday balloons and banner. On the wall to the side of where he sat a shelving unit had been cleared of ornaments, ready to display the many cards he would soon be opening, alongside his lovely gifts. Having been confined to his room for so many weeks, he was, naturally, somewhat confused at all the goings-on. When I told him, 'It's your hundredth birthday today, Dad! You always said you thought you'd see the hundredth and, God bless you, you have!'

'Who – me? A hundred?' He looked puzzled.

'Yes, you, Dad! You're a hundred years young today!' I replied. We smiled at one another, so happy in the moment.

During the next couple of hours, Lydia kept texting me from America, pointing out that, London being eight hours ahead of Seattle, she and Patrick wanted to know when it would be a convenient time for them to sing 'Happy Birthday' to Granddad William. I kept having to text back that either he was asleep or I had popped out to collect the food for the buffet. Finally a text came from her when I was at my dad's side and he was awake, so I told her, gleefully, 'You've timed it perfectly. I shall now put my mobile next to Granddad William's ear, and you and Patrick can start singing to him.'

'Dad,' I said, as I placed my mobile within his earshot, 'this is a lovely surprise for you. It's Lydia, your granddaughter, and her husband, Patrick, telephoning from America, to wish you happy birthday!' Dad smiled up at me, and reached out his hand to hold my mobile closer to his ear, and, as he did so, I heard the oh-so-heartwarming words, 'Happy birthday to you . . .'

Just as I was thinking, My goodness! It sounds as clear as if they were in the same room as us, I noticed the amazed looks on the faces of two cousins, Jenny and Pam, who were sitting opposite us, gazing open-mouthed at something behind me. I turned. There, strolling towards me, arms outstretched, singing their hearts out, were Patrick and Lydia.

All those texts had been a ploy, just in case it had entered my head that they might make it from America. Well, it had certainly worked because I hadn't had a clue. Their wonderful surprise visit put the icing on the cake. The CD player was switched off as Patrick, a great musician in his own right, entertained everyone with his guitar playing and singing.

It was also wonderful to have Klerry and her

boyfriend, Ben, there. The other residents of the home and the carers filled the day room, more than welcome to join in the celebrations. Patrick was a great hit with everyone, his kind nature shining through as he chatted with the 'golden oldies'.

Among the many celebratory birthday cards, there was one from Sir Iain Duncan Smith, then secretary of state for work and pensions, and, of course, a personally signed one from Her Majesty Queen Elizabeth II, both having pride of place on the shelving unit.

And so it was that my beloved dad's wish to 'see the hundredth' was fulfilled, as was mine that it would be as happy as it could possibly be.

I'm Forever Blowing Bubbles

On the 18 March 2012, Dad suffered yet another heart attack. I sat with him every day, and some nights, for the next three months. He slept eighty per cent of the time, which spared him from hours of confusion and despair.

By now, the majority of his contemporaries had gone, so, aside from me, only a handful of people came to visit him. Of those, four had a two-to-three-hour round trip to Dad's home yet they came regularly. I will be eternally grateful for their unwavering kindness and support at a time when it was needed more than ever.

At 6.20 p.m. on 29 June 2012, my beloved dad passed away.

Stephen took me in his arms. There were no words to comfort or soothe me. He knew how much I loved Dad.

On a few occasions when Dad and I had been walking around town and we'd seen a horse-drawn hearse in a funeral procession, he'd stop, doff his hat and say a prayer. When it had passed, he'd put his hat back on and point to the horses. 'Isn't that lovely?' So, for Dad, I organized a horse-drawn hearse with two magnificent black steeds, complete with black plumes. They were called Midnight and Star. I picked a coffin with an image of the London skyline by moonlight, which Dad loved so much, and a floral tribute to sit on top in blue and yellow. Dad had often told me about the moment he'd first seen Mum at a local dance. *She was the prettiest girl in the room, and as I watched her swish her blue and yellow floral dress, I knew she was the girl I would marry.* Dad would have loved that final nod to Mum, the love of his life, as he went to meet her in Heaven. I wrote the eulogy and asked the priest to read it word for word, and chose songs that Dad had loved.

The day finally arrived. I wore black trousers and a black top with pretty orange flowers around the neckline, which Dad had told me was his favourite. It suddenly brought to mind little Teddy waiting for me in his bed of marigolds. As Stephen, the girls and I set off, I was certain my feet and heart were filled with lead, so heavy was the weight of my grief.

I cried during the service until a particular song played. Then my tears stopped, and I smiled. *I'm forever blowing bubbles . . .* As the notes of Dad's favourite song rang out, the air above us was transformed into a cloud of bubbles. The bubble machine I'd ordered for the service was doing its job, and the mourners at the funeral smiled in memory of my beloved dad. In the light, colours and soapy bursts near my face, I could have sworn I saw his face, his beaming smile.

As we made our way outside, the clouds were thick and dark, and it was pouring with rain. I thought it was lovely. The heavens were crying. Despite the weather, the funeral director brought the bubble machine out to

Dad's graveside, and as my beloved dad was interred, the bubbles flew up and around us. Stephen, the girls and I released four white doves, and as their beating wings pushed them up and away, the most beautiful flash of colour broke out above us. High in the sky was the stunning arc of a rainbow.

After the funeral, I went to see Mamma Rosa. Her arthritis had stopped her attending but now, as I sat with her, her grief was so raw I could practically taste it.

As she wept, I said, 'Mamma Rosa, Dad wouldn't want you to cry like this for him. He's not suffering any more.'

She wiped her eyes. 'I'm crying for your dad but I'm crying for another reason too.'

Alarmed, I pulled my chair closer to her and took her hand. 'What's the matter? Are you ill, Mamma Rosa?'

She shook her head. 'Now that your dad's no longer around, I'm worried I'll never see you again.'

Maybe she thought I wouldn't want to see her because the retirement complex reminded me of Dad, but that couldn't have been further from the truth. 'Of course you'll see me again. You're like a mum to me and I'm not going to lose you, too.'

I visited twice a week, taking her jellied eels and the flowers she used to enjoy from Dad. Now his armchair was empty, and my heart lurched whenever I saw it, but I didn't let on to Mamma Rosa. I sat on that chair and felt his presence.

At home, I was struggling to cope with Dad's loss.

Nothing seemed to bring me any comfort until, one night, Stephen had an idea. 'Why don't we go away for a while?' Then he explained his thoughts. It was with the end goal in mind that I booked an appointment with my GP.

Three months later, armed with prescribed tranquillizers and pills to control my tummy, I boarded a plane and flew to Greece with Stephen.

I took the plunge and boarded a plane to Greece!

On the flight, I kept my eyes shut and gripped Stephen's hand. It was one of the hardest journeys of my life, but when the plane touched down and we disembarked, I felt the autumn warmth all around me.

Stephen hired a car and drove us through the mountains, up and up until, finally, we pulled up outside a villa, with wavy tiles and a lovely garden tucked behind a wrought-iron gate with lions on top.

'Are we here?' I said.

He nodded.

'It's beautiful,' I said, gazing at our rented holiday home.

'And it's ours,' Stephen replied.

I stared at him and, probably for the first time in my life, I was speechless.

He smiled his handsome smile, took my hand and led me into our new holiday home.

The property was in Yiala, Salamis, about sixteen nautical miles west of Athens, at the top of a picturesque mountain. Stretching down below us was what looked like a toy village, so pretty and perfect. There were mountains to either side, and to the left, the Aegean Sea twinkled and shimmered in the sunshine. It was a world away from gloomy London, which, when we'd left in the early hours, had been covered with fog and chilled us to the bone.

Through the wrought-iron gates a marble path led to the house. On the left a raised flowerbed was full of red and coral hibiscus, and on the right an assortment of flowers were growing in an even bigger bed. At the end of the path, a right turn took us behind more flowers, under a roofed walkway and down a flight of white marble steps. We were greeted with a never-ending stretch of bougainvillaea, layered with mauve and lilac blossoms. It was so beautiful, I couldn't find the words to tell Stephen how I felt.

He held my hand tightly, carefully helping me down the little staircase to a lower garden, where I was assailed by the smell of fresh oranges and roses. Pink rose bushes led us to a mini orchard with orange trees, tangerines, lemons, pomegranates, grapefruit, pears and figs!

I was blown away. 'Is this all really ours?'

'Yes,' Stephen replied, 'but wait till you see what's up there.'

By 'up there', he meant at the top of the main staircase, central to the house and leading to the 'front' door, which, actually, was at the back of the property. We climbed it together and I found myself on a white marble veranda. It was huge! On one side was the sun lounge, which linked to the front garden and entrance, and on the other a patterned glass door went into the living room.

But before I could go inside, I turned to take in the panoramic view we had of the mountains and the town below. It literally took my breath away. There, the veranda swept outwards, above the garden, supporting a long oval marble table.

More stairs took us to the upper apartment. On reaching a big wooden door, Stephen pointed to the bell and, with a great big smile, said, 'You've got to ring this first.'

I obliged and a chorus of birds tweeting rang out. I couldn't believe it. It was a real recording.

Inside, I found a fully stocked bar, a gorgeous lounge, with a three-piece suite, a nest of glass tables and silk flower arrangements on the coffee-table.

The bathroom was plush with black and white marble and a semi-circular bath.

A double bedroom overlooked the sea and another, with two single beds and a small balcony, had a view of the mountains. Back downstairs, and across the veranda, there was another living space and an open-plan fully fitted kitchen.

Our bedroom had fitted wardrobes and a bathroom. A separate lobby area led to more bathrooms and bedrooms, overlooking the veranda. There were fireplaces in the rooms – and more beauty than I could have imagined in a million years. I moved through the house, through the sun lounge and on to the veranda, shaking with emotion. My goodness, how lucky I was to be married to Stephen. I sank into a comfy chair and looked out to the sea.

Now, with archways overhead and the tang of orange groves in the air, I was reminded of Mrs Young's words all those years earlier. The medium had said, *You will come to be in a hot country, in a white house with arches, some place where oranges grow. After that, you will get better.*

Could this holiday have been what she was talking about?

Over the next few days, it became clear that she had been right. To be in Greece after all the difficulties of the last few years was a tonic for the soul – my soul. My anxiety dropped away and, for the first time in as long as I could remember, I slept soundly through the nights.

That holiday was like a rebirth in more ways than one. For fifty years, I'd been living pretty much within the confines of a two-mile radius. But in Greece, Stephen and I drove through the little villages or within a stone's throw from the sea and I could get out of the car at any time to take in the fresh sea breeze. Wherever we went, there were no yellow lines, or parking restrictions, so we could stop as and when we pleased.

After a month, we returned to Morden and I felt like a new woman. Life seemed to be moving along on a cloud. We returned again and again to our holiday home in Greece and it was there that I made friends with Heidi. One day we were chatting in the lane near our home when she asked Stephen, 'Can I borrow your wife tomorrow? I have a surprise for her.' She winked at us.

'Of course!' he said.

The next day she picked me up and, as I strapped myself in, she said, 'Now, Linda, you've taken me into your confidence and told me about your panic attacks. Today I have a treat in store for you, but if your tummy starts to feel funny or you feel like you can't catch your breath, please tell me. Okay?'

I felt a bit embarrassed.

'Don't worry,' she said. 'It's only me.'

I nodded. *What was she up to?*

Heidi took me to the Corinth Canal and to Loutraki, a place full of natural waterfalls. We stopped for lunch there, and then we were off again, driving and driving till the sun began to set. When we got home and Heidi stopped the car, she said, 'Linda, do you know what you've accomplished today?' She pointed to her dashboard. 'You've gone two hundred and eighty miles without a twitch of nerves or a panic attack.'

My gosh, I thought. In that moment, I realized how much I was capable of and it was a real turning point. All the times people had been unkind and told me to get over my anxiety for my children's sake seemed irrelevant now. It was like the world had been given to me on a plate and now I was invincible!

No matter what time of year we made the trip out to the Greek villa we called our Eagle's Nest, one thing stayed the same: the abundance of stray dogs and cats.

The dogs were wary and scared but the cats sauntered into our garden whenever they liked. I bought a decent stash of dog and cat food and had bowls at the ready for whichever creature dropped by for a chat.

Cinderella

It was shortly before Christmas 2009 and I had spent a happy day decorating our sitting room in Greece in readiness for the festivities to come. A large Christmas tree filled one corner, almost touching the ceiling, while a nativity scene and various other Christmas ornaments gave the room its festive cheer. I had pinned Santa's jolly face to one wall, and whenever its sensor detected motion, it shouted, 'Ho-ho-ho! Ho! Merry Christmas!' Once its latest victim had got over their fright, they collapsed into giggles.

Decorating the tree had taken the longest time and I was exhausted – not only because there were so many ornaments and baubles to be strategically placed but because our adorable black and white kitten, Cuddles – thought to be of the Turkish Angora breed – was trying to scamper up the branches. Time and again, I lifted her down. I didn't want her hanging among the baubles in case she was caught up in the wiring of the lights. However, with the agility of a mountaineer attempting to reach a summit, Cuddles repeatedly conquered our Christmas tree.

Every time, the baubles shimmied and shook until a few dropped off, whereupon I had to pick them up and put them back. Meanwhile, Cuddles took pride of place on the summit. I could have avoided all the havoc she was wreaking by shutting her out of the room, but I could no more deprive her of enjoying Christmas than I could a child. Our kitten *was* like a child to me.

I had come across her only recently while I was driving along a row of seaside restaurants. She was such a tiny kitten and she was sitting, her head hanging, looking so sad and forlorn on the roadside that I had to pull over. I asked the owner of the nearest restaurant if she belonged to her. 'No. Nobody wants her.'

I was out of my car like a gunshot. I scooped up the tiny ball of fluff. 'Well, here is someone who does!'

With that, I got back into my car and popped the kitten into the top of my sundress. She stretched her little legs out and looked up at me, as if to say, *Thank you for wanting me.*

She promptly laid her little head against my chest and fell into a contented sleep. As I looked at her snuggled up to me, I christened her Cuddles, wished her sweet dreams and set off for home.

When I reached the house, Stephen came out, as he always does, to see if I needed help with the shopping I had gone out for. Except I had no shopping. He stepped back from the empty boot and raised a quizzical eyebrow. Whenever I returned home without having completed my designated task, Stephen instantly knew something was up. Now he waited for an explanation.

I stepped towards him and pulled the top of my dress down a bit. He glanced round, quick as a flash, to make sure nobody was watching, then peered down my top. He let out a surprised chuckle. Just as my heart had melted when I'd set eyes upon Cuddles, so did Stephen's. Cuddles woke that afternoon to find she was double-blessed with love.

Now, having let Cuddles wreak havoc on my tree, I held her securely in my arms and admired my – our – handiwork. My thoughts turned back to those childhood Christmases when, year after year, my dreams of being given a puppy had stayed unfulfilled. I had been lucky enough to receive many beautiful gifts and I had been grateful for everything Mum and Dad had bestowed on me. But the burning desire for a puppy of my own had never left me.

By now, it was late in the evening so I headed to the patio doors, pausing to check whether Cuddles wanted to join me on the veranda. Well, she didn't. She jumped out of my arms and I headed to the comfy garden furniture we'd set up. By day, the house had a breathtaking view, and by twilight, it was simply magical. That night, a full moon was shining amid a blanket of twinkling stars and the Aegean Sea was shimmering calmly in the moonlight. The lights from Aegina, an island close to us, sparkled like jewels in a crown, joined occasionally by the lights of slow-moving cruise liners in the distance. The houses dotted around the mountainside were adorned with Christmas illuminations. Flickering lights spiralled on to verandas and rooftops, tipping downwards and creeping into homes through open windows. It was reminiscent of a scene from all those fairy tales I'd read as a child.

I sat in a balmy breeze, drinking in the spectacular dreamlike view, the peace and tranquillity only occasionally interrupted by the hooting of an owl. *Bliss.*

I had just taken a sip of chilled white wine when all of a sudden I was aware of a black and white flash. It shot into the lower garden, sped along past the roses and the orchard and up the staircase right on to the veranda, where I was sitting. It skidded to a halt two feet away from me. The flash was a Springer Spaniel. She stood rooted to the spot, her hair on end and shaking from head to paw. Her big brown eyes fixed on mine searchingly. *Are you friend or foe?*

I rose from my chair and walked slowly towards her, hunched over to make myself seem smaller and less threatening, while reassuring her quietly that she would be quite safe with me. The closer I got to her, the less she shook and her darting eyes took on a look of relief. In that moment, I felt it was true what people said, that dogs sense things around them.

I knelt down and held out my hand to her, as Dad had taught me all those years ago in Ramsgate. She nudged it and I began stroking the top of her head and her back, where I realized to my horror her tail had been lopped off! I was aware of the barbaric practice of chopping the tails off hunting dogs, but I knew it had long since been banned in Greece.

Now it became painfully apparent that this poor little mite had suffered the trauma rather recently. God help me if I ever found out who that cruel person was!

Now that this frightened creature was a little used to

me, I picked her up and sat down on the comfy chair with her on my lap. I whispered to her, stroking her head, ears and back. I glanced through the window and into the living room just in time to see the clock on the wall strike midnight. 'Cinderella,' I said. 'Welcome home, my darling.'

On my sixty-fifth Christmas, I had the gift I'd wanted for so many Christmases past – a real, live dog of my own – finally arrived? I continued stroking Cinderella and she rewarded me with licks on my hand. Whenever her eyes met mine, I felt a jolt of love trill through me. She soon fell asleep and, not wishing to disturb her, I stayed sitting with her on the veranda right through the night, only moving to wrap the blanket I had placed around my shoulders to cover both of us.

When day dawned, I gave Cinderella some breakfast. She couldn't eat it fast enough. As I watched her, I said, 'Where did you come from, girl? What have you been through?'

Whatever the answers, it was clear she'd spent many days without rest, food or drink. I contacted a local vet, Pavlos Pezaros, who, even though it was Christmas Day, said he would see her.

Stephen came into the kitchen and was about to say something to me when his jaw dropped at the sight of Cinderella. 'I know,' I said. 'I'll explain when I'm back from the vet.' I rushed out of the door, as Stephen called, 'Merry Christmas!'

We had no sooner arrived at the surgery than poor Cinderella seemed to lose all her fight. The vet came in and I handed her to him. 'Please help her.' He whisked her away for emergency surgery.

What if she was seriously ill? I'd only known her for a few short hours, but already I was devoted to her. Like Teddy, she had become a part of me from the moment I'd clapped eyes on her. I paced the floor manically.

Finally, the operation was over and Pavlos came into the waiting room. I rushed towards him and he held up his hands. 'She is okay, she is okay.'

I let out a breath I hadn't realized I'd been holding.

'But if you had not brought her to me now, Cinderella would definitely have died. She needed a hysterectomy.'

My eyes stung with tears and I couldn't stop them spilling over. Some were tears of sorrow for how poor Cinderella had suffered, and the rest for why nobody had helped her sooner. How had my poor dog found the strength to climb up that mountain and to our villa? Whatever her past, one thing was certain: I would never let Cinderella come into harm's way again.

Pavlos warned me that she had lost a lot of blood and her recovery was not certain.

For the first time in a long while, I closed my eyes and began to pray. *Please, please, please let Cinderella live. I'll give her a happy life and she'll be very well taken care of. Please let me bring her back to life – a real life – so that she can experience being properly loved.*

She needed to be kept in the recovery room for four days, but Pavlos kindly said that I could visit her every day when he went to check on her and feed her.

I didn't sleep a wink and returned to the veterinary clinic in good time. When Pavlos arrived, I didn't need to say anything. The look on my face did all the talking for me.

He led me inside, through the door at the back of the waiting room into the recovery room. The cages were empty, except for one. Inside, a familiar face was snoozing, her little head resting peacefully on her paws. I didn't want to disturb her but I couldn't help myself. 'Cinderella,' I whispered.

Her eyes opened at her name and her head lifted. She shuffled forward and pushed her nose to the bars. I placed my middle and index finger on top of her nose and stroked softly back and forth. If she could have wagged her tail, I knew she would have done so. Instead, she pushed against my hand, motioning for me to continue. I didn't have a tail to wag but my heart was doing flips. 'You're going to be just fine, my darling girl,' I told her.

Cinderella was kept at the surgery to recuperate, and I visited every day. It was clear she was getting stronger. By the fourth day, she was on her feet and her eyes were bright.

Finally, I was able to take her home. She trotted out of that surgery as if she was walking along a Chanel catwalk in Paris Fashion Week. She was so pleased with herself and had a new lease of life.

I took her home and gave her home-cooked chicken and vegetables. Then I showed her to my side of the bed I shared with Stephen. Next to it, on the floor, I put a soft pile of duvets and throws. Cinderella circled it, sniffed it, climbed on and slumped down with a huff. Cinderella was home. And from that day forth, I've called Pavlos 'Ayios', the Greek word for 'saint'.

Although Christmas was over, I wasn't going to let Cinderella go without. While Stephen looked after her, I browsed the shops for Christmas gifts in the sales. I bought her a paw-patterned plush dog bed, squeaky toys and chews to get her teeth around. But the main gift I had set my heart set on was most likely to be found on the other side of town. I drove across to the children's store, parked and went in. An assistant asked if she could help me. I told her I was looking for bedding with a *Cinderella* design. While there were umpteen different storybook themes available, there was none of *Cinderella*. The assistant, assuming I wanted it for my granddaughter, tried to persuade me to buy another design and showed me Snow White and the Seven Dwarfs dancing across a divan. 'I am sure she would enjoy this one just as much.'

I held back a laugh. If only she knew who this special gift was for. 'Thank you,' I said, 'but it has to be *Cinderella*.'

She shrugged her shoulders in defeat. At the next shop I tried, my luck was in. I paid for the *Cinderella* items and raced home to wrap the presents in lovely dog-patterned paper. I had also bought Cinderella tree gifts, including Christmassy headbands, with the words 'Merry Christmas' lighting up between them.

Whether they were for her enjoyment or mine, it wasn't clear.

By now, word had spread of our gorgeous new addition to the family and Klerry had used a courier service to deliver presents to Cinderella. She had sent a stocking full of dog toys and treats, and there was a package from Mamma Rosa. As I lifted out the Santa hat and peeped inside, I couldn't help but smile. Mamma Rosa had filled it to the brim with doggy treats. I tipped them into a box, except for one, and went towards Cinderella. I crouched down in front of her. 'I'm just going to try something, girl.'

She sniffed excitedly around me.

I said, 'Are you listening?'

She tipped her head as if to say *yes*.

I put my hand out. 'Paw.'

Cinderella stared at me and her eyebrows pushed upwards. *Is that it?* She placed her paw in my open hand and swished her stumpy tail. I laughed and gave her the treat. 'Who's a clever madam, eh?'

She'd indulged me with one thing, and I wondered if she'd indulge me with another.

While Cinderella was engrossed in the toys Klerry had sent for her, as well as for Cuddles, I took the opportunity to slip Cinderella's reindeer-ears headband, which I had bought, behind her ears. She didn't flinch! While some dogs dislike having anything put on their head, Cinderella seemed to enjoy it, not least because of all the fuss that came with it.

*

Cinderella needed six weeks of follow-ups with Pavlos and, slowly but surely, she fully recovered. Stephen and I took her for short walks along the quiet road where we lived and I was in my element. I thought back to all those happy walks I had taken with Teddy in my childhood, and of all the dogs I had met over the years who had made me yearn to have one of my own. My dream had, at long last, come true.

Cinderella was my right-hand girl. If I was in the kitchen preparing lunch, she'd sit beside me. If I was on the computer, she'd lie down next to me. She was the same in the garden and I soon learned that she wasn't interested in playing with a ball or running around. She was calm and quiet and only wanted to be beside her mum, which suited me down to the ground.

She slept happily in our bedroom and never disturbed me. In the morning, when I woke and got out of bed, she'd trot around behind me. Cinderella was my shadow. Soon I realized she had not been brought to me by Santa Claus but by God Himself, as my beloved dad's last gift to me from Heaven. I offered Him and Dad my heartfelt thanks for making my dream come true.

Some weeks later, Cinderella came with me in the car to the local bakery for some fresh loaves. On seeing some stray cats across from the road, I gave them some food and water – I kept a supply in the boot of my car. A nice young man I knew happened to be in the shop, and when he came out and saw Cinderella sitting in my car, he called, 'Have you got a dog now?'

I nodded. 'You'll never believe how that one came to find me,' I said. As I told him how Cinderella had arrived in our garden and moved into our hearts, his eyes widened. When I'd finished, he told me something, and now my eyes popped. He explained that Cinderella had been bred in England as a gun dog and his father-in-law – whom I didn't know – had bought her to retrieve the birds he shot.

'So you know Cinderella?' I said.

'Yes,' he said, 'but her name is Atalanta.'

I learned that while she had been out on a bird hunt with him and his father-in-law, Cinderella had suddenly disappeared. 'We thought she'd been stolen,' he said. He looked at me seriously and I stared right back at him.

'Well, it's a good thing that you know I'd do no such thing,' I said.

He placed a hand on my arm. 'I know how much you love animals, Linda, so don't worry, nobody is implying anything.'

I let out a breath as he pointed to the mountain across the landscape below us. 'All the way over there, that's where she disappeared,' he said. The area he was pointing to was miles and miles away. From our joint calculations, we worked out that Cinderella had been lost for a month before she'd found sanctuary with me. With this new information, it was even more of a miracle in my eyes that Cinderella had survived.

The young man continued, 'I have to tell my father-in-law you've found her.'

I nodded, a knot of anxiety tightening in my stomach.

The young man paced with his mobile phone to his ear, waiting for someone to answer. I went to the car, where Cinderella sat with her face sticking out of the window, her tongue lolling out. I stroked her head. 'Atalanta, was that your name?' Momentarily, she bristled.

I had no doubt her previous existence had been miserable, prompting her to flee from her life as a gun dog. Knowing her as I now did, I was sure she would have hated that hectic, noisy existence. She belonged with me, where she was finally enjoying a peaceful, happy life. Anger rose in me when I thought of how the signs that she'd been ill had been cruelly ignored for so long. I opened the door and, cautiously, she stepped out. I crouched down and hugged her to me. She didn't move, just rested her head on my arm.

Twenty minutes later, a battered red pickup truck pulled up. A bulky man got out and headed towards us. He had a mean face and deep creases in his brow – he'd obviously spent a lifetime frowning. He was the opposite of my father, who had had creases that ran from nose to chin, either side of his mouth, for all the hours he had spent smiling. The man shoved a stack of papers in front of me, and on the top was a photograph of a familiar little face. 'Atalanta,' he said, tapping the picture, then pointing to Cinderella.

The paperwork showed ownership. I handed it back, unsure what to say. Though the man could not speak any English, I could tell he was cold-hearted. How could any owner ignore beautiful Cinderella, now waiting patiently by my side, after having lost her more than two months ago? He didn't so much as reach out to stroke her or show her any affection. It told me everything I needed to know about him.

It was clear that all he cared about was getting her back to work for him but I had no intention of letting her go. He began speaking in Greek, hotly debating Cinderella with his son-in-law. He didn't know that I had a good enough grasp of Greek to catch the gist of the conversation. When they fell silent, I told him the one thing that really mattered. I wanted to keep Cinderella.

The young man told the older one that Cinderella had been very ill and I had paid a lot of money to Pavlos to help her. It was likely she would need ongoing medical care.

That seemed to put him off: he began to waver in his desire to seize Cinderella from me. I silently urged the young man to continue in that vein, as it had obviously touched a nerve.

And so he did.

'The dog will likely cost you a lot in the future. It will prove expensive.'

I took the opportunity to stress that I didn't need to be paid back. 'I just want Cinderella,' I said. The older man grunted, nodded, and handed me her papers. Then, without so much as a glance at Cinderella, he got back into his truck and sped off.

I thanked the young man and climbed into the car, shaking. I had come so close to losing Cinderella. Within seconds I was off towards home, where Cinderella would be safe.

I couldn't figure out if it was my own anxiety I was feeling, or Cinderella's in the passenger seat beside me, for she was shaking too. *Poor sausage*. She must have hated that man. I put my hand towards her slowly, not wanting to startle her, and she nudged it with her nose.

She didn't look at me. Instead she sat bolt upright, her eyes on the road, staring straight ahead. Straight for home.

For weeks after my nerve-racking encounter with that man, I was bumping into his relatives. Each and every one thanked me for taking Cinderella. I had a strong feeling they all knew he had not been good to her. I thanked them for their kind words and reassured them that Cinderella could not be more loved or better cared for than if she were my own flesh and blood.

One relative didn't beat around the bush: 'Linda, her previous owner is a horrible man. He was so cruel to Cinderella and he used to beat her. My family is so thankful to you for saving her from what would have been such a miserable existence.' Her joy and relief at Cinderella now being in my care came tumbling out.

As complimentary as her words about me were, I couldn't help wondering why her family had not saved the dog themselves. I couldn't have stood by and watched that dear little soul suffer as they had. Now I knew how poor Cinderella had suffered, I wouldn't have been surprised if she was unapproachable, but she was quite the reverse. She was a sweet, loving, friendly girl, and everyone who met her adored her – none more so than me.

Almost six decades had passed since I'd waited outside the department store to talk to Santa in his grotto about my Christmas wish for a puppy of my own. Finally, my lifelong dream had become a firm reality. Cinderella was here to stay!

Back and Forth We Go

With Cinderella now part of our family, we had her microchipped and vaccinated. Now that she had her own pet passport, as Cuddles did, she could fly with us between the UK and Greece. But home is where the heart is and she loved Greece best of all. I'd take her for a drive through the villages and down to the sea. On the way, she'd sit in the passenger seat next to me on her pink pet blanket. She wasn't a noisy girl so usually she'd sit there quietly, resting her nose on my right thigh – until I spotted something I thought she'd like to see. 'Look, Cinderella! Look at all those sheep out there.'

She'd sit bolt upright, have a snoop out of the open window, then lay her head on my thigh again.

Sometimes I'd sing to her. She usually listened without objecting, but whenever I sang 'She'll Be Coming Round The Mountain', she'd sit up with a funny look on her face and tilt her head away from me. If I could have read her mind, I would have bet money that she was thinking, *That's my mum*.

After driving for a while, we'd stop at a taverna where I'd have a coffee and she'd lap at a bowl of water. Before long, we'd have an audience of children who wanted to know all about her. I did my best to tell them in Greek that her name was Cinderella and the story of how she came into my life. She was very patient with the little hands that reached out to stroke and touch her.

But Cinderella didn't like being in busy places or walking among lots of people, like at a market. I took her to the quieter villages or to the beach, where she could roll around in the sand and dip her toes into the sea. Not that she'd go far from my side. She was usually stuck to me like glue. Just the way I liked it. And sometimes when I gave her belly a 'chubby rub', as I called it, she gazed up at me with a disbelieving look in her eyes, as if to say, *Did I really find you?*

Every time I told her, 'Yes, my darling. You really did.'

Some time later I was visiting Heidi when she asked, 'Have you seen my baby?'

Well, it was no secret that both of us were well past child-bearing age and my eyes must have done the talking for she laughed. 'Look into the garden there.' I stood up and looked over the balcony. There, gazing up at us, was a gorgeous yellow Labrador puppy. 'We're already looking after a lot of strays and can't afford to keep this one,' she explained.

I went down to the garden and held the puppy to my face. 'How would you like to come and be loved by us for ever?' He licked my face and that was it. I didn't need to consult Stephen, who was beside me. We were always on the same wavelength.

We took him home, where Cinderella sniffed him and circled around him. Then she grabbed him by the scruff of the neck, took him to her bed in our room and cuddled him to her side. 'Who's a lucky boy, then?' I asked, when I found them.

And Stephen said, 'Lucky Boy.' He was christened.

With Cinderella being so compact, I had no expectation of how quickly Lucky Boy would grow. One minute he was digging up my geraniums and the next he was flirting and chasing Cinderella around, hoping perhaps to get Lucky. Not that she minded his advances. Whenever she'd been for a haircut, she'd sidle up to him, lick his cheek and rub herself against him. The minx! Although Lucky Boy was the larger of the two, Cinderella was very much the boss. She had her favourite spot, in her bed beside mine, but sometimes she'd fancy Lucky Boy's armchair. She would go to Lucky Boy, comfy in his chair, and let out a *WOOF*. Being the gentleman he is, he'd duly vacate the seat and let her have a turn while he took her usual spot in her Burberry bed. Later she'd go up to him. *WOOF*. He'd get up and return to his armchair. They did make me laugh.

When it came to tricks, Lucky Boy was much savvier. I'd call them both to my feet and tell Lucky Boy to shake hands. He'd reach up and paw at the air so I'd hand him a treat.

Then I'd tell Cinderella the same. She'd stare at me blankly and Lucky Boy would repeat the action, gunning for another nibble. 'I'm talking to Cinderella,' I'd tell him. His paw would return to the floor and he'd resist the urge to lift it again when I gave Cinderella the command. Ten seconds would slip by and, finally, she'd offer her paw.

Stephen adored the dogs as much as I did and took Lucky Boy on twice-daily walks.

Cinderella would chase after them, her ears flying. I'd hear Stephen shout, 'It's a good thing this isn't an airport run, Cinderella. You'd be taking off by now!'

Whenever I went shopping, I'd return to two noses sticking through the gate; my welcoming committee, I called them. Cinderella and Lucky Boy would circle around my feet and, when they finally calmed down, wait for their favourite treat. I'd tease them a bit, then say, 'Come on, then! Chubby rubs!'

They'd roll on to their backs, tongues lolling out, and wait for me to tickle their tummies.

At the end of it all, though, Cinderella was a mummy's girl and Lucky Boy was a daddy's boy. Like any good parent, neither of us showed any favouritism. When Stephen was wandering around the garden or going out for a stroll, he'd shout, 'Come on, my boy! Come with Daddy, my girl.' Two dogs would follow.

If Cinderella didn't fancy it, she'd wait beside me until Lucky Boy signalled his homecoming with a *WOOF* at the gate. Then she would motion for me to follow her and lead me to the gate, while Lucky Boy stood on the other side waiting for Stephen to catch up. Cinderella would stare at me. She was waiting for permission. I would, of course, say, 'Go on then, give him a kiss.' She'd close the gap between them and lick him lovingly.

In time I realized it was not just Lucky Boy and Cinderella who were coming into their own. The anxiety I'd been suffering from almost all my life had gone. Travelling no longer seemed an issue. Somewhere in the process of bringing Cinderella back to life and love, I'd come back too. I talked to Cinderella, often late into the night, telling her about Mum, Dad and all the years I'd longed for her. 'I had a special friend called Teddy,' I told her. 'He was a dog like you and I loved him dearly.' She listened carefully as I told her about the special times I'd shared with him and she rested her nose on my lap.

It was in that moment that I understood something about myself. Though I had been lucky enough to find the love of my life and have two darling daughters, until now, with Cinderella, I hadn't felt complete. The loss of Mum, Dad and all the others I'd held close to me had left a gaping hole in my chest for the longest time. Somehow Cinderella had filled it.

Now I have an oh-so-special best friend to call my own. She and Lucky Boy give me unconditional love and never sit in judgement. Whenever we're in Greece, our roof seems to bristle and shine, miaow and purr. At any one point, there are around thirty stray cats roaming around the villa, be it on the roof or the veranda or in the sunshine among the lemon trees. We've named some of them, including Bon Bon, Love and her friend Kisses, a tabby called Bubble and her buddy Squeak but, really, it's hard to keep track.

Our vet has a theory that word has got round the

animal kingdom: our house will supply them with food, water and love.

Perhaps that's true, but what has definitely come true is Mary Young's prophecy about my being surrounded by animals.

But however they hear of us, there's always room for more at the Steliou inn.

Now, as I pen this final chapter, Lucky Boy is snoozing to my right and Cinderella is on my left. Cuddles has taken her usual spot on my lap and is purring ever so quietly. Just as these three animals needed a fresh start, I have experienced a rebirth along with them. Together, we have our own little piece of paradise.

Acknowledgements

To Daniel Bunyard, publisher, Penguin Books: little did you know when you wrote to me, then telephoned to thank me for my entry into the true-story competition, organized by *Take a Break* magazine and Penguin Books, that you had come to my rescue. Over the past few years, I'd had to watch too many of my loved ones suffer from major illnesses, then try to cope with the grief of their loss. Following the passing of my beloved dad, and my best childhood friend on exactly the same day, 29 June 2012, all the anxiety culminated and I fell into a deep hole of depression. I had wonderful understanding and support from my closest loved ones and felt guilty that, no matter how hard I tried, I was incapable of climbing out of that hole. Then, Daniel, you came along, as if in answer to my prayers. With your praise of my 'way with words', your help and encouragement, I came to know that 'getting it down on paper' is indeed therapeutic. I had to focus on my writing, for several hours a day, for months, so you provided me with the best therapy of all. Now, with my book complete, I'm back to my happy-go-lucky self. God bless you, Daniel.

To Punteha van Terheyden, senior feature writer for *Take a Break*: you have given me so much of your valuable time, patience and thoughtfulness, and have encouraged me with your faith in me. Thank you, also, for making me a part of your life. God bless you, Punteha.

To my dearest husband Stephen: being the quiet unassuming person you are, you didn't want me to mention you in my book. Probably because you realized that I would want to write an encyclopaedia in praise of you and you would be so embarrassed if I did. I had to include you because you are my life. But, in respecting your wishes, I shall simply say here that you are the most wonderful husband, father, son, son-in-law, brother and all-round best friend that anyone could ever wish for. Please don't feel embarrassed: credit where credit is due. I thank God every single day for his having blessed my life with you. God bless you, Stephen.

To our daughters Lydia and Klerry: my sincerest heartfelt thanks to you both for all your encouragement. You are such an important part of my story. God bless you both.

To our son-in-law Patrick: you are more like a son than a son-in-law to us. You have brought so much joy into Lydia's life, but into ours also.

For my cousin, Laraine Macinnes: the amount of practical help, hospitality and emotional support you have so kindly given me over the past couple of years has been invaluable. Your being there for my beloved dad and for me at the very time when he was most in need of sincere love and support is appreciated far more than any amount of words can ever say. And for your continuing concern over my welfare and your enthusiastic encouragement for my writing this book, equally my heartfelt thanks and gratitude. God bless you, Laraine.

For my cousins, Jenny Corpe and Pamela Knibbs: not only is it lovely to see two sisters as incredibly close as you two are to one another, but I feel honoured that you treat me as a third. When it comes to matters of the heart, it is as though we are of one mind. Our shared love of dogs, especially our very own four-legged family, is a strong bond between us. That you regularly and frequently travelled a long distance to spend such quality time in support of my beloved Dad, during those awful last nine months of his life and in doing so you were also there for me, is appreciated beyond words, and I thank you both from the bottom of my heart. Your wonderful stories of what your four-legged family have been up to have shed so much welcoming light after those dark days, and it is a joy I hope will also bring sunshine into the lives of my readers. God bless you, Jenny and Pam.

For Kay and Andrew Eleftheriou: well, what can I tell you that I haven't already? In the relatively few short years that we have come to know one another, it is amazing how very close we have become, isn't it? I feel as if we have known one another for ever and, not only that, have become closer and more caring about one another than some people who are of the same flesh and blood. We are on the same wavelength, where so many things are concerned. We have the same interests and always love spending quality time together whenever we can; always having a laugh and a joke and thoroughly enjoying one another's company, in which we feel totally at ease and at home. Over and above everything, the amount of time and emotional support you put into being there for my dad and for me was incredible. You are a prime example that it is not always a case of blood being thicker than water. And, for your continuing to be such an important part of my life, spurring me on with writing this book and encouraging me every step of the way, I thank you from the very depths of my soul. God bless you, Kay and Andrew.

For Alan, Joyce and Sam Fleming: how blessed Dad was to have you as true friends, and how blessed am I that you have extended the pleasure of your friendship to me. In spite of your own advancing years and health problems, the fact that you took the time, trouble and effort to travel a long distance, and frequently, to visit him over the last few years of his life speaks volumes of how much you cared for him, as he did for you and as I do. And how very welcome and at home you made me feel when I visited you, and had the bonus of meeting your beloved black and white Border Collie, Sam, of whom you spoke so highly. As, sadly, you were unable to have children of your own, Sam is just like a son to you. I remember your telling me of the day when you went to collect him from a farm: the farmer brought him out by the scruff of his little neck and told you, 'If he's no good, you can bring him back.'

Me, meeting Father Christmas in 1947.

My mum, Bett Peck.

Walking with my mum and my beloved godmother, Ann Mason.

My dad, Bill Beck,
in his care home with
Mamma Rosa.

A father is someone
who lifts you up and
holds you there forever

Celebrating his
hundredth birthday.

Our daughters, Klerry and Lydia, with our beloved goddaughters, who were named after them.

I spent the happiest eighteen years of my career working for dear Dr Jock Smallwood.

One of the views from 'The Eagle's Nest', our villa in Greece.

Lucky Boy.

Lucky with his adoring dad, my dearest Stephen.

Cinderella, Lucky and Andrea the tortoise.

My 'welcoming committee', waiting at the main gates of our home to greet me!